Zen to reveal the extraordinary Tao

Trevor Rufli

New Sarum Press
UNITED KINGDOM

Publisher's Note

This publication is designed to provide accurate and authoritative information in regard to the subject matter covered. It is sold with the understanding that the publisher is not engaged in rendering psychological, financial, legal, or other professional services. If expert assistance or counseling is needed, the services of a competent professional should be sought.

For Sharon, Adam, Daniel and Jill

Copyright © 2023 Trevor Rufli
Copyright © 2023 New Sarum Press
First published by New Sarum Press, August 2023
www.newsarumpress.com

ISBN 978-1-7397249-8-6
All Rights Reserved

Contents

Introduction vii
Acknowledgements xi

Chapter 1—Zen points to the extraordinary Tao .. 1
    The impossible what 4
    The impossible where.. 6

Chapter 2—Your head is full of *you* 9
    Try this witnessing meditation exercise........... 10
    Choose a distancing technique to do this........ 11
    Try a further distancing method 11
    Conscious awareness and self 12
    Separateness and permanency 13
    Our vulnerable self.. 15

Chapter 3—A startling discovery 17
    The illusion 18
    Why we can't see it 19
    Illusion of separateness.................................... 20
    What is self then?... 24
    Who we are really 24
    Outrageous discovery 26

Chapter 4—The enlightenment quest................ 27
    Dual consciousness... 27
    Non-dual consciousness 28

CONTENTS

The Eastern quest 29
Zen Buddhism 32
Satori 33
Minor satori 35

Chapter 5—The self that can't stop desiring 37

Desire 37
Identifying the process of desire 38
What happens when we satisfy a desire 39
The bucket and the banquet 43
Why can we not fill up? 45
The realisation of fulfilment 47
Applying the understanding 48
The Tao that desire cannot find 50

Chapter 6—The self that can't stop doing 51

Identifying doing 51
Doing is a dynamic of our restless self 53
The doing that keeps us away from the Tao 54
Applying the understanding 56

Chapter 7—The self that cannot know the present moment 59

The missing aspect of time 59
The present moment that self cannot know 62
The illusion of time passing 64
The eternal now 64
Now is the only moment 67
Experiencing deepening moments 69

CONTENTS

Chapter 8—The path to enlightenment ... 71
- Zen and direct pointing ... 73
- Bodhidharma ... 74

Chapter 9—The seeking that takes us away ... 77
- Seeking in time ... 78
- Seeking what we cannot know through knowledge ... 79
- Seeking through ideas that always have opposites ... 83
- Seeking to know a movement that cannot be contained in an idea ... 85
- Seeking out and away from where it is to be found ... 86

Chapter 10—Seeking what we already have ... 88
- The paradox that we already are enlightened ... 88
- Unclean words ... 89
- The rightful protest ... 90
- The Tao is so close ... 91
- Giving up seeking what you already have ... 92

Chapter 11—The Tao and our existence questions ... 94
- Is there a God? ... 95
- What about death? ... 97
- The illusory fear of death ... 98
- What about free will and predestination? ... 99
- What is the meaning or purpose to our life? ... 101
- The meaning and purpose we overlook ... 103

CONTENTS

What is going on? 105

Chapter 12—Walking with the Tao 108

The Tao and the suffering of self.................... 109
Balanced seeking 111
The Tao shines on self 112
The I that is we 114

Chapter 13—Beware of false paths.................. 117

Caution: adopting an enlightened outlook 118
Caution: acting like a spiritual person 118
Caution: forcing spontaneity 119
Caution: interfering with our thoughts 120
Caution: following the path of acceptance 120
Caution: practicing detachment 121
Caution: suppressing the self......................... 122
Consider meditation....................................... 122

Chapter 14—Peace comes dropping slowly 125

How peace might come 126
Travelling light 127

Endnotes and Citations 130

Introduction

Is there more to life than just this? Is there some meaning or some purpose to our existence, a higher order or a God of some sort? If you are reading this, then you have probably asked the very same questions that I was asking myself about 30 years ago…

I remember how, back in these earlier years, through various readings, I began to come to understand and know something extraordinary that has—in an unexpected way—answered these questions. And this understanding, this 'knowing', has brought freedom, peace and sometimes a sense of joyous excitement. Many other things flow from this knowing and even at times when a mood state would obscure the knowing, there was the awareness that the knowing is just around the corner.

Life is difficult: we all find it so. We find ourselves on this planet without any idea of what life is about or where it is going. We are so psychologically vulnerable. Whether it is things on the outside we need, or good mental health on the inside, we need so much to have peace and happiness. Life is unpredictable and as is evident when we look around us, it can at times be extremely harsh but at other times it can be benevolent and a joy. Knowing something which seems greater than our individual existence makes adversity and times of despair much easier to manage. We can come to know something that will always endure no matter what life throws at us.

The really wonderful thing about this knowing is that it is not something we need to come to know through acquiring knowledge, becoming religious, doing spiritual stuff, making an effort or doing anything in particular. You don't have to believe anything either. Rather this knowing is acquired through a process of understanding that is a process of letting go rather than accruing. It is something that can be gained by standing in the same spot, doing nothing, unencumbered by anything. And when you get it you don't even have to change your life!

In my youth I read books on religion, philosophy and psychology. Then I came across the less religious, more spiritual philosophies of Buddhism (Zen Buddhism in particular) and writings on the Tao. These Eastern approaches turned everything on its head for me and set everything in the opposite direction to where I had been looking. What I really want to communicate to you now is that this was not about my becoming a Zen devotee or a Buddhist or anything like that. What I was coming to know and understand belonged to the psychological domain— transpersonal psychology as it is now referred to in the West. The extraordinary *thing* that is to be known and understood can be neatly summed up by the word *Tao* and this is what I will be referring to throughout this book.

When we know the Tao we have spiritual enlightenment, the common goal of Eastern religions. The great thing about using the word Tao is that it is unconfined and so does not narrow our focus in any way, leaving room for all that we want to explore.

So regarding the question: *Is there more to life than just this?* I am tempted to say: *Yes, there is, I promise, I have found something, it is real.* But so many say this and so often such promises leave us disappointed. Obviously, I really believe there is something extraordinary and wonderful to know, something that can add a new and deeply fulfilling dimension to our lives. But it is wiser not to be persuaded of this by someone else; <u>only believe what you find for yourself.</u>

It has always been a challenge to communicate the central message of Zen while also bringing an awareness of the Tao. It's almost a matter of 'either you see it or you don't'. Have you ever seen those 2D pictures where you look at it, look and look, and sometimes you just see the surface, and then in a moment your perception relaxes and you see deeply into the picture, you see into its deeper nature in full 3D. It's a little like this. The words are read and they can be mildly interesting, but then sometimes they produce a break into a deeper seeing. Or more usually they are read and there is a sense that they are pointing at something that can't quite be grasped, there is an inkling of knowing, enough to make you follow the trail.

If you are an experienced seeker, you may have found a certain obscurity in many books on spirituality or Eastern mysticism. Writing in the area of spiritual psychology is difficult, it's so easy to misinform. It is very easy to give advice that ties seekers' minds in knots rather than bringing the experience of freedom.

What I offer in this book are pointers to sparks of *knowing*, profound insights that go beyond the intellectual level. If we need a term for how this book works it is similar to the Zen method of 'direct pointing' where you are 'pointed' towards the heart of the matter. And when you are you may be brought to a deep spiritual awareness of something extraordinary. The awareness is potentially one of connection, belonging, joy, excitement, peace and perhaps, most of all, freedom. And one spark of knowing is all you need:

For this one rare event,
Gladly I would give a thousand coins of gold!
With a hat on my head and a bundle at my side,
On my staff I carry the breeze and the full moon.

Author unknown
quoted in Alan Watts, *The Meaning of Happiness*

Acknowledgments

I owe a debt of gratitude to authors and explorers of the inner Self. Rather than clutter the text with academic-style citations I list below those to whom I have made most frequent reference in the text.

Blyth, R.H. (2021) *Haiku*, (Zenrin-kushu). Brooklyn, NY: Angelico Press. Three volumes comprising Spring, Autumn/Winter and Summer.

Chuang-Tzu. *Chuang-Tzu* (Tr. Martin Palmer) 2006. London: Penguin.

Goddard, Dwight (2009) *A Buddhist Bible*. Knoxville, TN: Wordsworth Classics.

Linssen, Robert (1994) *Living Zen*. New York, NY: Grove Press.

Tzu, Lao. *Tao Te Ching* (1999)(Tr. S. Mitchell) London: Frances Lincoln Publishing Ltd.

Watts, Alan. (1948) *The Spirit of Zen*. London: John Murray. (1968) *The Meaning of Happiness*. London: Rider. (2021) *The Way of Zen*. London: Rider.

Thank you to my publishers, Catherine and Julian Noyce of New Sarum press, for their professionalism, clarity and overall for being such a pleasure to deal with.

Chapter 1
Zen points to the extraordinary Tao

Zen points to the Tao
– Zen is the finger, Tao is the moon

ZEN BEST POINTS THE WAY, WHILE THE TAO BEST describes our destination.

And so we must first start with the tantalising question, *what is this extraordinary Tao? What is this wonderful thing that we can come to know that will bring us inner peace?* If we could answer the question with an easy clarity, then perhaps we could also come to know the Tao with some simplicity. But this is not the case. Trying to describe the Tao or the nature of Zen is difficult. It is difficult not because the Tao (or Zen) are too complicated or too philosophical. Not at all.

One way to define the difficulty in describing the Tao, is to say that it is too broad. It is too broad for our limited minds to grasp. For one thing the Tao is infinite and we know how the concept of infinity is too broad for us to conceive of. When we consider something going on and on forever, infinitely, we reach a limit to our thinking. We can't relate to it.

It was the spiritual seekers of the East who 'discovered' the Tao. When it came to seeking something more to life they went *in* where in the West we went *out*. We went 'out' and sought a God through belief systems, faith-based scriptures, we tried to build a relationship with an external God, a God who was 'out there'. In the East they sought a God by looking in, into themselves, deep into their experience of conscious awareness. The Buddha said: *Be a light unto yourself* and they did; they went right back to the source of their looking. What they found was a spiritual source that was very different to the idea of a God out there. They found something that not only included us but also was not separate from us in any way.

Eastern religions, of which there are many, each with many different schools, have different names for this search for the source of our being, or enlightenment. For example, we have Buddhism where enlightenment is to attain the state of *nirvana* and in Hinduism it is to merge with *Brahman*. In Taoism it is to be in harmony with the Tao. So in this book when we refer to the Tao we are also referring to what it is that the various Eastern religions have discovered, the same thing, a unity beyond our normal limits of consciousness.

Now, before we explore the nature of the Tao, it may be useful to give you a brief history of Taoism and Buddhism, as this book draws on their writings the most. I say 'brief' because you can find extensive information online. I must thank Dwight Goddard's *Buddhist Bible* for facts and insights about Buddha's life. The word *Tao* is used by the Eastern spiritual system of Taoism which has its origins in ancient China around the sixth/fifth century BC. Tradition has it that Taoism was founded by Lao Tzu, who left behind him a work called the *Tao Te Ching*. This extraordinary little book, consisting of eighty-one short chapters, formed the basis of the spiritual school of Taoism. Later figures, particularly Chuang Tzu, through his work the *Chuang-Tzu*, extended the ideas of the *Tao Te Ching*. The spiritual psychology of Taoism emphasises insight and understanding as a *way* to inner freedom. To this end it advocates the use of meditation, surrender to the rhythms of nature, enquiry into the mysteries of the human condition and our place in the cosmos.

Buddhism too originates from the words of one individual, Siddhartha Gautama, universally known as the Buddha. He was born in India around 560 BC. He is said to have achieved Buddhahood, or 'enlightenment', whilst sitting in meditation under a tree known as the Bodhi Tree. His teachings from this day on formed the basis of Buddhism. He claimed that Buddhahood could be achieved by following the *Noble Eightfold Path*. Buddhism has since then diversified into different schools. Zen Buddhism is the school that is most closely aligned to the themes in this book. It is not at all religious and it advocates the use of meditation and 'direct pointing' to discover our spiritual source.

So now you know some of the history. I could also

have given you a history of human consciousness, for knowing the Tao, experiencing enlightenment, is above all a psychological quest and it is a quest that is for everyone. We do not need to become a Buddhist, Hindu or Zen master. (It is equally available to the person next to you, the account executive, the person in prison, the millionaire, the person living on the streets and to you yourself.) So what is it?

The impossible what

In trying to explain what the Tao is in a straightforward way I can say that it is:

>   the substance of the universe
>   the basis of everything
>   the totality that is everything
>   the all-embracing origin of all things

Now as you consider these descriptions you will see that you are really being given very little information. There is nothing to get a grip of in these descriptions and I might as well be saying that *everything is everything* or *all is all* or even *blah is blah!*

And this is the problem in trying to describe what the Tao is. It is trying to say something about what is a universal essence that is the source and the manifestation of all that exists. A Zenrin poem says something of what kind of word we might need to describe the Tao:

'the Tao that can be described in words is not the real Tao'

*One word settles heaven and earth,
One word levels the whole world.*

R.H. Blyth, *Haiku*

So the Tao is not just the source of things but it *is* all things. And in trying to grasp this concept we find ourselves in a peculiar position for we cannot conceive of all things without excluding ourselves from that same category, excluding ourselves from all things. When we say, for example, that the Tao is all of reality, it seems to mean that we experience ourselves as being a witness to that reality. And we are in this position for the simple reason that we are aware of it. And so in describing the Tao we cannot express just how inclusive it is because it is a concept that must always be separate from you, the thinker, the one who is aware, the separate outside observer. Can you think of a concept or an idea that is not being thought of by you? To do this you would have to come up with a concept into which you would disappear!

Now you have just read something that is confusing, you can't quite grasp what is being said. A concept into which you would disappear? It doesn't make sense and there is also the suggestion that you are, somehow, getting in the way of understanding what is being said. You are right to be confused. This confusion has been brought about by Zen direct pointing, a pointing at a something that doesn't make sense to *you*.

The impossible where

If we are coming from a Western perspective, we would probably try to approach this question in the same way that we might have thought about our idea of God. The Judeo-Christian perspective teaches us about a God with whom we can have a relationship and that same God is to be found in a place other than where we are. Even if we think of this God as being within us, we still regard God as being in a place that is separate from us, some place that we can relate to.

In considering where the Tao is we must look in a very different direction. Our usual direction of search has probably been out and away from where we are now. We have searched around and outside our source. In a way we can say that our searching has been one-dimensional. We search out and across in a horizontal direction. If we are to find the Tao we must look in another direction altogether and it is a most difficult one to point to. It is not so much about pointing inward to ourselves but inward to a deeper aspect of our inner experience. And to find it we must not look out and around about us, rather we must go back to the source of our looking.

As you now wonder where it is, look around you and consider that it is all that you are seeing. The *Tao Te Ching* describes:

ZEN POINTS TO THE EXTRAORDINARY TAO

The great Tao flows everywhere,
All things are born from it,
yet it does not create them.
♡ *It pours itself into its work,* ♡
yet it makes no claim.
It nourishes infinite worlds,
yet it does not hold onto them.

Lao Tzu, *Tao Te Ching*

You might now say: *Well either it is nothing special or I am not seeing it.* Both of these conclusions would be correct. The Tao is nothing special because when it is known you are still seeing the same ordinary things. But you are seeing these things in an entirely new way, from a wholly different perspective. When the Tao is seen it is not what we see that changes but the *see-er* that changes. Our experience of everything around us stays the same but it is the experience-er that changes, *we* change. There is a change at the centre of our awareness and this change is extraordinarily special. This is why we can say that the Tao is not hidden because it is what is right before our eyes.

Yes, it is right before our eyes and yet it is extraordinarily well hidden. We do not see it and so it seems that we must be in complete isolation from it because when we have searched we have found nothing. It is so well hidden that even those who have seen it have had great difficulty in showing or describing to us where or how it is to be found.

It may be difficult to believe that, as we live

our lives in isolation from the Tao, we seem to live a surface existence that has us skimming across a hidden depth containing a vast richness. And this is not overstating it. But how can this Tao, this spiritual dimension to our lives that is in front and behind us every single moment be so well hidden from our view? Right now we cannot see the Tao because there is something very definitely blocking it from our experience, from our view. The Eastern mystics have sought the means for us to remove this block from our awareness.

What is blocking the Tao so effectively from your view is you! The very *you* who is wondering what this means!

Chapter 2
Your head is full of *you*

THE END OF THE LAST CHAPTER LEFT THINGS SOMEwhat cryptic to say the least. *You* are an obstacle: *you* get in the way of knowing the Tao, *you* get in the way of spiritual enlightenment! So what exactly is it that is in the way, what do we mean by this *you*? What is being referred to is your essential experience of *I*-ness, in other words your essential self. A good way to get a sense of this is to say your name out loud. When you say your name there is a sense of you, a flavour of you, a sense of you in the background and separate from all that you experience. Now consider the following:

Who am I? *— use as a gatha meditation*

- *I* have a body, but *I* am not my body.
    My body can be damaged, *I* could lose a part of it, but *I* would remain. *I* am aware of my body, *I* can direct my body, but *I* am not my body.

- *I* have sensations such as physical pain and pleasure.
    > These sensations change. *I* am aware of these sensations but *I* am not these sensations.

- *I* have emotions such as shame and pride, happiness and sadness.
    > These emotions change. *I* am aware of these emotions but *I* am not these emotions.

- *I* have a personality, but *I* am not my personality.
    > My personality can change. Sometimes *I* can be outgoing and other times not. *I* am aware of my personality but *I* am not my personality.

- *I* have thoughts but *I* am not these thoughts.
    > These thoughts come and go. *I* am aware of the flowering and fading of these thoughts but *I* am not these thoughts.

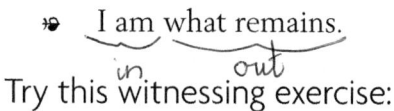

- I am what remains.

Try this witnessing exercise: (in. / out)

- Allow your mind to wander where it will:

thoughts of now, past or future, worried thoughts, happy thoughts, time pressure thoughts.

> As you are aware of whatever it is that is passing through your mind:
>
> consider that the essential you is separate from these thoughts.
>
> Imagine that this essential you is silently witnessing the goings on in your mind:
>
> from a very quiet and detached corner of your mind.

Choose a distancing technique to do this:

> Imagine that everything that goes on in your mind is passing by on a great big movie screen.
>
> All that you experience, all the contents of your awareness, your thoughts, feelings, images, sensations are all passing by on this screen.
>
> The essential you is sitting back and simply observing all that is on the screen. The real you is sitting in the audience quietly watching the show. You are completely separate from it and can watch in a detached way what is going on.

Try a further distancing method:

> Imagine that you are the person who is

observing yourself who in turn is watching the show.

This is what is meant by 'self', the essential *I*-ness that can silently witness all from a silent corner of your mind.

Conscious awareness and self

You will notice that this silent witnessing of what is happening on the screen is only momentary, if you do get a sense of it at all.

You cannot actually maintain the experience of not identifying with the mind's activities—you are immediately absorbed back into what is happening on the screen.

This screen is our conscious awareness, it holds all that we are consciously aware of.

Consider the screen again. It is full of *stuff*, full of awareness of thoughts, emotions, sensations, memories.

What else do you notice? What is missing from this description?

It is full of *I*, full of 'self'. "I, me, mine" is the constant refrain.

It is infused with the flavour of self. It is always *my* thoughts, *my* feelings, *my* happiness, *my* sadness, *my* body.

The I-centred consciousness is what we call this present evolved state of consciousness. It is also referred to as our dual consciousness where we have two fundamental experiences in our awareness. One is the experience of 'I' and the other is the experience of the contents of our awareness—thoughts, feelings, images and so forth—everything of which the 'I' is aware.

Much of the time our sense of *I*-ness merges with the contents of our awareness—those thoughts and mental contents that we tried to view on the screen.

By this I mean that we are usually lost in our thoughts, on automatic pilot much of the time.

Our experience of *I*-ness can be strongest when we are doing a witnessing exercise as we just did. Then we have more of an experience of the pilot at the controls, the thinker thinking the thoughts, the feeler feeling the feelings. However even when we are lost in our thoughts or feelings we can still say, '*I* am thinking such and such, *I* am feeling such and such'.

For the purpose of this exploration and what follows in this book, 'you', *I* and 'self' refer to exactly the same thing. So the word 'self' again is referring to your *essential observing I-ness* and not 'self' as it is used in self-development psychology where 'self' includes your personality, thoughts and feelings. I will occasionally use the term 'I-self' to remind us of this.

Separateness and permanency

There are two fundamental experiences that accompany our sense of *I*-ness: separateness and permanency.

ZEN POINTS TO THE EXTRAORDINARY TAO

Our experience of separateness makes it feel as though we are in *here* and life is out *there*.

> We listen through our ears and see through our eyes.
>
> We think our thoughts and feel our feelings.
>
> We can direct operations.
>
> We can decide what we want to think about and what actions we want to take.
>
> We feel ourselves to be separate from time: look at the second hand of a clock: it seems as though we can *see* time passing by.
>
> Our separateness is experienced as being separate from all of reality.
>
> We experience our I-centred awareness as distinct from the contents of our awareness.

We feel a sense of permanency within this experience of separateness.

> Our thoughts and emotions change constantly.
>
> We can lose parts of our body.
>
> We can lose some brain cells and memories.
>
> Our *I* that is aware does not change.
>
> Our *I*-ness is experienced as a still, permanent and unchanging centre around which all

of reality, inner and outer, is in a constant process of change.

Our vulnerable self

Having a sense of self, of I, of me, means we can easily feel under threat. Of course we do: we have so many things to protect.

Again, say your name out loud, that's who is vulnerable.

We feel the need to protect our image: our likability, our self-esteem, our position, our power, our money, our possessions—the list goes on.

We feel the need to protect the extensions of self, the other things with which we identify: our family, our friends, our religion, our country our favoured sporting team. When things don't go our way we experience negative emotions.

This sounds like persistent negativity, but a balanced view tells us that our life can be going well and our self can feel good and strong in the world.

> So this is what is being referred to as self or *I*-ness. Our essential *I*-ness feels independent, separate and permanent from all our experience and it is also infused in all our experience.
>
> *This* is the self, the *I*, the *you* that gets in the way of your experiencing the Tao.
>
> *You* get in the way of experiencing a deep

peace that lies within.

You are in the way of your own spiritual enlightenment!

But all is not as it seems, there is a startling discovery to be made about *you*!

Chapter 3
A startling discovery

FIREWORKS SHOULD GO OFF AS YOU COME TO THIS new chapter; here you will find a revelation that is, well... big!

The revelation is that the self that we identified in the previous chapter, your essential self, your experience of pure *I*-ness, the fundamental experience you have of *you*, is a total illusion.

Yes, your experience of *I*-ness is not real! The famous Buddhist doctrine states:

> *Suffering alone exists, none who suffer;*
> *The deed there is, but no doer thereof*
> *(Nirvana is, but no one seeking it;*
> *The Path there is, but none who travel it.)*
>
> Alan Watts, *The Way of Zen*

We will get back to these astounding words later.

Not only have Eastern mystics known about the illusion of self for centuries, they also discovered that *it is the very illusion of self that hides the Tao*. In other words, it is the illusion of self that is the block to spiritual enlightenment. Yes, it is our experience of that *I*-ness which stands in the way of enlightenment.

This central realisation of the illusion of self led to the formation of Eastern religions. Some of the terms used for the doctrine of no-self are (*anatta* in Buddhism and *advaita* in Hinduism) Seeing through the illusion or experiencing the dropping of the veil of self is the spiritual goal that aspirants seek in order to achieve enlightenment.

The illusion

Now before you try and struggle to see through the illusion, you should know that there is no way you can see through it. You can't even get a glimpse of it.

Our experience of self feels so real and fundamental that it is no wonder we have never questioned it. Note again that when we talk about the illusion of the I-self we are not talking about your conscious awareness. We are referring to your experience of *I*-ness, the flavour of you, that permeates your consciousness awareness.

There is no need to struggle to gain particular clarity on this, let the ideas land softly and further chapters will help to create the conditions for clarity to develop.

Consider now, what is an illusion? An illusion is when we perceive something and think it is real, that the thing has substance, where in fact it does not. Like a mirage of trees and water in the desert which vanishes when the thirsty wanderer approaches: whilst the experience of it was real, on closer inspection it had no permanency or substance. This is the same for self. If we could approach it in some way we would find that it too has no permanency or substance.

You might now reasonably say: *Ok, so self is an illusion, it has no permanency or substance, but it is the experience I have of me and I am stuck with it, what's the big deal, what's the big reveal?*

Well yes, but hold on a minute. No permanency or substance! NO PERMANENCY OR SUBSTANCE! This *is* a big deal. You experience self as something permanent, separate, unchanging, of substance and something to protect at all costs. And this is the outrageous confidence trick. What you spend your whole psychological life protecting, what is at the centre of all your psychological vulnerabilities, all your psychological suffering, is not really there at all!

Not only is self not really there, your experience of self is actually *not even necessary to your functioning.* On the contrary, it greatly limits your functioning. What you experience as fundamental and so necessary to your psychological functioning is baseless and redundant.

Why we can't see it

So why can't you see through the illusion? To understand this, consider the desert mirage again.

The mirage is real, so illusory or not, it is real in our experience. However, when we look closer there is nothing there. Similarly, the mirage of self is real, so illusory or not, it is real and of course central and fundamental to our experiencing (at our current level of consciousness).

Now here is the tricky bit. Can we say: *When we look closer there is nothing there?* No, we can't really say that. And this is the problem, for the mirage would be looking at the mirage! We can't see into the illusion of ourselves for the illusion is also the looker and we can't get away from that. No matter how hard you try to see it, no matter how much you twist and turn in your mind, your position of duality (of two) always contains a sense of *I*-ness. As the Zenrin poem states, we are:

> *Like a sword that cuts but cannot cut itself,*
> *Like an eye that sees but cannot see itself.*
>
> R.H. Blyth, *Haiku*

We cannot look into our source for we are the source of our very looking. For now let us consider some of the contradictions that having a sense of self gives.

Illusion of separateness

As you read this sentence you are aware of both the sentence and of yourself reading it at the same time. You are aware of a stream of experience that contains the words you are reading and any other thoughts you may be having. There is the *you* observing this stream of experience and you can think: *I am reading such and such*. And this is our position of duality, there is *I* on the one hand and the experience of what is being read on the other.

Now, consider where is the experience of *you* in all this? Is it the case that there are two streams of experience flowing through your awareness, one the awareness of yourself, and the other, the words you are reading. But then for you to be aware of these two streams of experience there would have to be a third stream of awareness, and so on. No, the answer is that there is only *one* stream of experience in your awareness. There is *no separate you* observing it. The experience of yourself reading these words is part of the same stream of experience that contains the words. There are not two streams of experience.

You are not separate from the experience. You cannot experience yourself reading and the words that are being read at the same time. It seems as though you can but what actually happens is that, in order to be aware of the experience of yourself reading, you must momentarily stop reading, and in that moment you have the experience of the thought or image of yourself reading. (Again, I want to thank Alan Watts in his book *The Wisdom of Insecurity* for his insights here).

This example does not just apply to reading. It applies to all of our inner experience. Our experience of *I*-ness is in the stream of all our experience.

We are never separate from it. We are fooled into thinking it because of the speed of our thought processes and their interaction with memory. Our experience of I-ness is a thought that is no different to any other thoughts that we have. Within our mind there is only one stream of experience. There are not two, there is only one.

Consider the witness exercise again. We noted in Chapter 2 that if you did manage to achieve the witnessing perspective it was only for a moment. It is not possible to maintain a sense of I-ness as separate from your experience because again, there is no *I* separate from your experience. It is all within the same stream of experience.

The reason witnessing can give a sense of separation is that, by saying to yourself you are not the contents of your awareness, you are not this not that, you experience a purer sense of self, detached from the contents it is usually infused with. But it is still just a thought within one stream of awareness, not as separate.

So really there is no-one sitting in the audience watching the show, there is only the screen of awareness containing various thoughts and experiences that you are having. Any experience you have of you witnessing what's on the screen is on the screen also. There is no audience, there is only the screen. There is no separate witness!

We are faced with our inner contradiction of self every time we use the word 'I'. When we are thinking or feeling something, we experience that '*I* am thinking such and such' or '*I* am feeling such and such'. In order to be aware of this we have to be in a witness position, but who is witnessing the witness of our experience? How does the self feel the feeling, how does the self think the thinking? So again, for this to make sense there has to be a witness of the witness and then a third, ad infinitum. It makes no sense. It makes no sense because there is only the thought, the feeling, the knowing, the seeing. There is no separate thinker, no separate one who feels.

Consider also what happens when we make a decision, do we decide to decide to decide ad infinitum. No, there is no self that decides, there is only the decision. Watch yourself next time you get out of bed, did you decide to get up or did you just get up?

I remember when I first read around this subject that I didn't quite get it, but there was an intuition that something was being pointed at that was significant. My first introduction to the area was *The Way of Zen* by Alan Watts, one of the earlier books introducing the concepts of Zen Buddhism to the West. This was back in the late 1980s when I was embarking on a career in psychology and I had been reading books on self-development and psychotherapy. This book was different.

Instead of being about the development of self it pointed to the *illusion* of self. I found the writings obscure, which was not surprising given the nature of the subject matter. However, I had inklings of understanding, little sparks of recognition that there was something being pointed at that was significant. And in these little sparks of recognition there was a sense that here were pointers to a new kind of freedom.

What is self, then?

So if self is an illusion what is this sense of I-ness of me-ness that is so fundamental to our experience? Yes, it is a mirage that has no substance. It has no permanency. It has no separateness. But *what* is it?

The mirage of self can best be understood as a tension within our awareness. We may think that this tension of self is fundamental and necessary to our functioning and psychological existence. But in a moment of 'seeing' we find that when this tension is released, the strain, the suffering of self, is simply gone. We see, or rather it is seen, that the tension of self is not fundamental or necessary to our functioning at all. Like a large crease on a sheet of paper, when we remove the crease we have smoothness and so too for self, when the tension is released we have smooth functioning and peace.

Who we are really

There is nothing enduring, continuous, solid or unchanging in you. There is nothing permanent or separate within. Your experience of self is just a

A STARTLING DISCOVERY

thought and a feeling amongst all the other thoughts and feelings in one stream of consciousness. There is not one point of consciousness observing the other, there is only one stream of consciousness. *we are Becoming*

Who we really are is *process.* We are a momentary experience amongst the always moving and changing stream of experience. The self is a thought that is born, flowers and dies in each passing moment— there is no underlying continuous entity of self, there is no permanence within us. In Buddhism the term for attaining the state of enlightenment is nirvana and it means extinction or blowing out, in the sense of blowing out a candle. In this context the Buddha described the impermanence, *anicca*, of the self as a candle flame passing along a row of unlit candles. The flame of self is extinguished on one candle before the next one is lit and so on. There is no connection between one candle and the next. The flame of self is impermanent. It has no continuity and is *recreated* moment to moment. What this means is that there is no connection between the you who was reading this a moment ago and the you who is reading it now, and now and now.

It may be daunting to consider that there is nothing stable or enduring within us. The idea that there is no grounding of self to our experience, no separate thinker of our thoughts can feel unsteady. But 'no you' does not mean we are empty, quite the opposite. When the self falls away we do not fall into an abyss. We fall into a greater unity that in Eastern literature is called the universal or Supreme Self.

Outrageous discovery

That there is no self within us is a remarkable and outrageous discovery. It is outrageous because our whole lives are spent in defence of this self that is an impostor within us. The self that is the cause of all our suffering is a sham, a con. Your experience of self that you spend a lifetime protecting and gratifying is a puff of smoke. Our life struggle has been to be somebody when there is no one to be in the first place. There is no one to be vulnerable, no *I* whose interests need to be furthered.

It is this tension of self, this puff of smoke, that is preventing us from experiencing the deep peace that lies within. When the illusion is seen through:

> *Meeting, they laugh and laugh*
> *The forest grove, the many fallen leaves*

R.H. Blyth, *Haiku*

Chapter 4
The enlightenment quest

THE DEEP PEACE THAT WE ARE TOLD IS WITHIN US; which one of us does not want this? Then we read, or someone tells us that it's our own essential identity, the impostor self, that stands in the way of our getting this peace. This is indeed an unexpected roadblock in our quest for enlightenment. It's frustrating, it's exasperating, but it's important that we understand this.

Dual consciousness

We referred to our consciousness as being dual (made up of two) in the last chapter. Dual consciousness describes our present unenlightened consciousness where we have a strong sense of *I* on the one hand while being aware of the contents of our awareness on the other. This is the consciousness we have but we don't want! It is our suffering consciousness, referred to as our *dukkha* consciousness in Buddhism. We have spoken about how the position of duality, where we experience self, results in our living with a sense of threat. We need so much from life, while life goes its own way oblivious to our needs.

In our human condition we cannot avoid being vulnerable, for there is no real foundation, no permanency or separateness, to our identity of self. No wonder we want to accumulate so much stuff, possessions, power, position, identities and the like. We want to fill ourselves up so that we may experience ourselves as being something solid and permanent.

Non-dual consciousness

Non-dual consciousness refers to the enlightened state, sometimes known as 'Buddha Consciousness'. We say 'non-dual', meaning not two, because at this level of consciousness the experience is of pure awareness, with no *I* that is separate from this awareness. It has been described as the experience of a greatly expanded identity with a broadening of our consciousness. When we move beyond what is found to be our little individual self, there is a tremendous sense of spreading out. The experience of self is one that loses potency; it fades into the background and is no longer our centre. Instead, our new centre is one that can be described as being both 'everywhere and nowhere'. There is no dominant, permanent and separate experience of self.

A good way to think about this is to consider a container of water with a very strong dilution of orange cordial. Now imagine that the water represents our conscious awareness and the orange cordial is the flavour of self. It's easy to see from this representation how our awareness is heavily dominated by self. Now imagine that you add many buckets, endless buckets, of water to an ever-expanding container. Consider how the flavour of self would get less and less and how conscious awareness would become purer, and more expansive. This could be compared with an enlightened awareness.

Think about how different our experience of the world would be from this perspective of non-dual awareness. Imagine that someone says something offensive to you: when you have no sense of self, or perhaps only a whisper of self, the insult would have nowhere to land. It would merely be information coming from a direction and there would be no self to meet it, take in or be triggered by it. Having no strong sense of *I* there would be no-one to be vulnerable, no *me* to be psychologically protected. In the non-dual state there is, rather than a sense of threat, a feeling of rightness and peace. The tension of self has been released. Other words that can describe the non-dual state are: unity, connectedness, merging, belonging, oneness, wholeness, harmony, tranquility, joy, bliss and love.

The Eastern quest

The spiritual quest that we associate with Eastern religions is of course the quest for spiritual enlightenment, moving from dual to non-dual consciousness. Gautama Buddha is a prime example of someone who achieved enlightenment and passed on his teachings. Different teachings have led to the formation of different religions and religious sects associated with them. Buddhism has hundreds of sects for example. There are also Taoism, Confucianism, Sikhism, Jainism and others, all with their different sects.

With so many religions and their offshoots, it is not surprising then that there are so many approaches to achieving the enlightened state of consciousness. Some approaches involve adopting religious belief systems but many of the approaches involve living a certain way of life. In Buddhism for example, as we mentioned earlier, there is the Noble Eightfold Path which sets out a particular way of life for its devotees to follow. The eight steps of the path encourage its followers to achieve perfection in the areas of perfect view, resolve, speech, conduct, livelihood, effort, mindfulness and concentration. Taoism encourages finding enlightenment in and through our engagement with daily waking life.

Many of us, whether we are seeking enlightenment or simply wellbeing, are familiar with meditation and mindfulness practices. Meditation, whilst originally used as a spiritual practice, has positive effects on psychological health and wellbeing, which have been well researched and verified [1]. Again, in line with different religions and sects developing, so too many different types of meditation and spiritual practices have developed over the centuries.

We could refer to the types of meditation used

in Buddhism, Taoism and Hinduism as the *spiritual* meditation practices. They are also used in some Christian and Jewish traditions. Here meditation is more focused on inner awareness and may include silent or chanted prayer.

Visualisation meditation is practiced in the Tibetan meditation school and in some Hindu approaches. The meditator focuses on a religious symbol or deity, with a view to quieting the mind and becoming imbued with specific attributes or qualities associated with the visualised object.

Chanting meditation is used by many spiritual traditions—a particular word, sound or mantra is repeated -over and over again.

Mindfulness meditation usually emphasises a focus on physical sensations or the breath. As different thoughts arise the practice is to notice these thoughts without judgement, and bring the focus back to the breath.

Focused meditation is another practice where we bring our concentration to focus on whatever activity is being engaged in. A good example of this is the influence of Zen Buddhism in the development of the Japanese tea ceremony. Here tea is prepared and presented in a very ceremonial way. You can do the same when you next make a cup of tea, quietly noticing every movement!

Movement meditations include *hatha* yoga (over 5000 years old), martial arts, Tai Chi and dancing.

There are also the methods of ritual focused

practices, breathwork techniques, fasting, painting, calligraphy, meditative gardening, meditative flower arranging, reading of scripture and classic texts.

You will notice that a common theme of these various methods is to try and lessen the influence of self by quieting or freeing the mind of thought. It is also the case that enlightenment can come through spontaneous awakening and sometimes through a psychological crisis that in some way brought about a collapse of self.

Zen Buddhism

I am giving Zen Buddhism its own heading here as it more closely resembles the approach we will be taking in these chapters. Like all the Eastern spiritual psychologies Zen uses the method of meditation: practitioners of Zen may also adopt ascetic practices, such as relinquishing possessions and limiting their diet. Zen differentiates itself from the other approaches in that it emphasises insight into the nature of mind, perceiving one's true nature. It does not concern itself with religious doctrines or belief systems, and some Zen schools have also been influenced by Taoism, which similarly does not engage with dogma or doctrine. You will already have read about the favoured method of Zen—direct pointing to the nature of the mind and you will learn more about this in later chapters.

Satori

The word *satori* refers to a non-permanent experience of enlightenment, of awakening, seeing into one's true nature. It is much more common to experience *satori* than it is to achieve the permanent state of enlightenment. It is also said that one needs to experience many occasions of *satori* in order to move to the enlightened state of Buddha nature, or non-dual consciousness as it has been described. The practice of meditation is well known for producing profound moments of *satori* and descriptions of these experiences are well documented.

Up to now we have discussed Eastern religions and used terms that derive from their particular systems. But of course, enlightenment and *satori* have not been limited to any race or religion. We are all eligible, so long as we have a consciousness! Moments of enlightenment or full enlightenment can come to us regardless of whether we are following a spiritual path or not.

In the West these experiences are referred to as mystic experiences, transcendent experiences or bliss experiences. Abraham Maslow, the humanist psychologist, called them 'peak experiences' or moments of 'self-actualisation'. Much has been written on these experiences and some of the descriptions are quite remarkable. The experience has been described as being of 'a veil being lifted from one's eyes' and of realising that 'one is surrounded by an incredible loving energy', and that 'everything both living and non-living, is bound inextricably with a kind of consciousness that cannot be described in words'. Another description recounts 'I seemed to be enveloped in a cocoon of golden light that actually felt warm, and which radiated a feeling of Love so intense that it was almost tangible. One felt that one could grasp handfuls of it, and fill one's pockets'.[2]

These descriptions have invited adverse comments about mental illness or drug use. Of course, drugs and mental illness can produce all sorts of experiences but these accounts are reported by people who claimed to be neither mentally ill or using drugs.

My interest in this area came out of a personal experience of—what should I call it? Maybe 'bliss' describes it the best. Although it occurred over 30 years ago, before I had read anything on Eastern religions, I have a strong and lasting memory of it.

I was reading a self-development book that was saying something about self-autonomy. I remember really appreciating something about being psychologically independent, maybe being independent and separate from thoughts and feelings. Then in an instant I experienced a mind shift where the sense of 'me' was released and, as the descriptions say, I found myself in a field of golden energy. I distinctly remember looking at the leg of a chair and I saw this energy rather than wood.

If I was to use a word for the feeling associated

with this experience it would be *Love*. I don't know why the word Love describes it but that was it. The whole experience was sudden and lasted probably only a few seconds. It has never been repeated. It was as if a hole had been punched in my consciousness and was then patched up really well! I remember shortly after sourcing a book on mystic experiences and it was this exploration that marked the beginning of my interest in the area of enlightenment and Eastern psychologies.

Minor Satori

Minor *satori* refers to a lesser but much more common experience of enlightenment which can still be very profound. Such experiences can also be described as moments of heightened consciousness or heightened awareness moments. They can simply be an experience of *isness*, that everything purely and simply *is* and of everything being perfectly okay. It appears that we move beyond what is found to be our limited individual self and there is a sense of expansion. One account describes it as like having a giant tooth extracted from the centre of one's being with the resulting peace and relief that followed. We can also experience everyday slippages of self where we feel carried away by the all-consuming rapture of music. For a moment we lose ourselves in it, we become it and we feel elevated. Similarly, when we are suddenly confronted by a panoramic view it seems that we transcend our usual boundaries of self in order to take in its beauty or vastness. There are many times in our lives where we lose ourselves in what we are doing, seeing, hearing or feeling and we experience a more expansive awareness. Sometimes, for no particular reason, we can just feel joyful and that everything is perfectly okay.

Such peak experiences are usually short-lived, but when they are more profound we can experience a deep peace and freedom. If we experience this we will know with certitude that within us there is a deep peace; that beyond our limited experience of self, our I-centred consciousness, we know we are part of something greater.

In the following three chapters we will come to understand how the illusory identity of self has kept us away from discovering this peace within. Our experience of self has deceived us and how we understand ourselves and our relationship with life and it has done this in three powerful and fundamental ways.

Deceptions of self have prevented us from finding true peace and happiness our whole life. We have been stuck on a treadmill, keeping ourselves away from knowing the Tao, away from the place that we really want to find.

Chapter 5
The self that can't stop desiring

Desire

DESIRE IS THE FIRST OF THE DECEPTIONS OF SELF THAT we will be exploring—and it is a big one! It is an inner craving that causes us to always seek *out* and *away* from where the Tao is to be found.

Consider the implications of this. What I am suggesting is that our actual *desiring* is preventing us from finding what we really want! It is our process of desire, whether it is for inner peace, enlightenment or for the many other more trivial things that we desire day to day, that is preventing us from discovering the inner peace that knowing the Tao brings. This is the deception of desire and it turns things on their head!

It really is a shocking statement to consider, that the inner process of desire that we have used all our life to guide us in our search for real happiness, has been leading us down the wrong path!

The problem of desire has always been central to the Eastern quest. In Buddhism, where desire (*trishna*) is regarded as the cause of suffering, great efforts have been made to solve the problem of this inner craving that we all have. Some mystics have attempted to stifle or kill their desires by depriving themselves as much as possible. These ascetics could be seen roaming the countryside existing with just a cloak and a begging bowl. In the Buddha's day asceticism was sometimes practiced to a severe degree and he is reported to have tried the approach himself but gave it up when it only led to his becoming emaciated and exhausted—and not enlightened.

Identifying the process of desire

We all know what desire is. Right now you may be desiring a number of different things. You are reading this book and probably hoping you can get something out of it and, as I write this my own desire is to express well what I want to say. Or maybe you are desiring to finish this chapter so that you can do something else. As your mind wanders you can see the process of desire, it moves from one thing to the other and it is usually focused on different future scenarios that you wish could come about. Or sometimes it is pulled into some memory from the past that you wish could have been different.

Our desiring is experienced as a recurring craving, or a feeling of emptiness and wanting, that focuses our minds on things that we think may make us feel better, happier or more at peace. In our consideration of desire here, we are talking about the process, the desiring, wanting, longing feeling

THE SELF THAT CAN'T STOP DESIRING

itself, rather than the objects of our desire, the things we want. And consider also that we are not talking about the desire for our basic needs of food, shelter and clothing. These are physical needs that we must fulfill to stay alive. What we are talking about is the process of desire that has us endlessly wanting for something—anything—that we believe we need to be happy.

In a way (and paradoxically) all our lives we have been trying to achieve the same thing that some of the great mystics strove to attain. We too have been searching for fulfilment by trying to get rid of our desires. The difference is that we have been trying to do this by feeding our desires whilst the mystics have tried to starve them. Neither has worked!

What happens when we satisfy a desire

We spend our energies trying to satisfy this empty desiring feeling inside of us. It seems that we do so because we believe in some way that satisfying desires is getting us somewhere, that we are becoming happier or more fulfilled as we go along. It is almost as though we believe that if we can just catch up on all our desires that we will come to a point where we will find peace and fulfilment.

When we examine closely what satisfying a desire has done for us we find that we always seem to end up pretty much in the same place. We look forward to getting something, or for a situation to change in some way. We do this believing that once we get what we want we will be happier or more fulfilled than we are now. Now it does feel good to satisfy a desire, most of the time, but we find that soon after getting what we want that we are desiring something else. If we think about it we can see that we repeat this process over and over again. And this is our life. We repeat this cycle of desiring, satisfying, and desiring again. Despite our best efforts we don't seem to stay fuller or more satisfied as we go along.

At first this may seem difficult to believe, for surely satisfying our desires has been increasing our happiness in some way! But consider for a moment where the last month, year, or ten years has got you. Has your hard work in satisfying your desires increased your overall feeling of happiness and fulfilment? Except for the removal of emotional suffering, it is unlikely that any happiness gained has been anything other than short-lived. It seems that desire and feelings of lack return soon after we have satisfied a particular desire. Think back to when you finally acquired something that you had been wanting for some time, something tangible like a new car or bicycle or new clothes. What happens to your desire after it has been satisfied? For a while you may be happy or excited about your new acquisition, but soon afterwards, sometimes almost immediately, you find your inner process of desire stirring once again. I remember watching a talk show where a multi-millionaire was telling of his admittedly ridiculous experience of having purchased a million-pound yacht. He was delighted with this new acquisition until he docked it beside a multi-billionaire's yacht that had cost something like twenty million. In that moment his previous satisfaction began to diminish and he felt his desire for a bigger yacht stir once again.

It seems that any satisfaction or happiness gained lasts only as long as the comparison between where we were and where we are now remains. Soon the satisfying comparison wears out and we find ourselves desiring something else, or an improvement on the latest acquisition. It seems that the newly acquired happiness vanishes soon after it appears and all we are left with is the memory of an experience which we may now want to repeat—an added desire! I am presently desiring to finish this chapter and when I do it will feel good very briefly, as my desire moves to finishing the next one. And of course, when I finish the book, yes guess where my desire will move to then!

The process is the same for non-material desires. Take our desire for success, for example. We can be pleased with a new job promotion; we may have more money, better self-esteem, but soon we find ourselves desiring to do well in the new job and it won't be too long before we find ourselves focused on the desire for another promotion. If we do well in sports, we find that anything other than an improvement on the previous achievement can seem like a failure. It seems that the higher we climb in terms of status or achievement then the greater is our desire to hold onto that position. The higher up we go the worse it is to fall and should we ever reach the top we may then fall foul of Lao Tzu's caution: *He who stands on tiptoe totters.* For even when we do manage to get much of what we want in life we can be left in the unfortunate position of feeling a vacuum, a vague emptiness. This comes from having nothing to fix our desires on. We want something but we are not sure what it is. It is because of this that one of Oscar Wilde's characters could remark: *In this world there are only two tragedies. One is not getting what one wants, and the other is getting it.*

Consider a time when you were very worried about something, bad health for example, and you thought if only you could be free of it you would be the happiest person in the world. We are the happiest person in the world until we forget our previous troubles, our desires resurface, and we begin to feel dissatisfied again.

Rather than becoming free from desire, we have become slaves to this powerful process within ourselves. Although we have so many more material goods than previous generations, it seems we desire now more than ever. We find ourselves living faster and faster and the fire of desire has only grown stronger through our fueling it. It seems that we have been running on the spot. And in no way is this our fault, we are all the same. It is our present-day human condition. At this point in our exploration, we can say two things about desire:

> Firstly, it seems that all our hard work in satisfying desires, whilst it might have kept unhappiness at bay, has done nothing to increase our overall level of happiness and fulfilment.
>
> Secondly, it becomes clear that we are as far away from being able to satisfy our desires as ever.

It seems that desire is a process all of its own. It is a process that burns up the objects of our craving just as a fire burns up the fuel with which we feed it. As the purpose of fire is to burn, the purpose of desire is: to desire without end. It is an inner force, calling out insatiably and endlessly.

So what is it that is going on inside us making our efforts to satisfy our desires so impossible? We will find that it is because our experience of desiring leads us to have a fundamentally flawed and false notion about ourselves and our relationship with life. It gives us what I would call a 'bucket and banquet' outlook on life.

The bucket and the banquet

Desire causes us to treat ourselves as though we are a bucket and life as though it is a banquet. Certainly not a very flattering view of ourselves but it does say something very important about a powerful misconception that we hold.

We regard the empty desiring feeling inside of ourselves as being like an empty place, like a bucket or a vessel that can somehow be filled up when we get something that we desire. And we believe that this something is to be found on the banquet table of life with its vast array of fillings. We feel as though we are empty on the inside and the filling is on the outside and that in order to fill ourselves up we must take that filling into us. When I say on the *outside*, I mean in a place other than where we feel our emptiness; I don't just mean physically outside us in the way we want a material item like a car; It could also be something in the mind that we want, such as greater self-confidence.

In our search for happiness we are fooled into thinking in this inside-outside way. But when we look at the situation more closely it is clear that, regardless of how many things we have been able to acquire, regardless of how many things we have been able to get on the outside in order to fill us up on the inside, we still desire as much as ever. This is true for us and it is true for others. The rich and famous are no closer to finding fulfilment than anyone else. In fact it often seems that outer success comes at the cost of inner happiness. We, the vessel that desires to be filled up, become no fuller as we take more in. No matter how much we take in it doesn't seem to fill our emptiness.

Why can we not fill up?

Desire is not the result of an emptiness inside that needs to be filled.

We cannot satisfy desire because our desire—our inner experience of something lacking—is not pointing to, nor is it representative of, a space inside of ourselves that *can* be filled up! Our experience of ourselves as having an emptiness that can be filled up is a deception. We are not like a vessel that can be filled. There is no container, no place inside us to receive the gains of desire. The emptiness that we feel inside is not a place or a space. There is no place inside us that can take in, hold onto and keep the gains of desire. There is no space inside us that is producing the feeling of desire.

What then is the emptiness that we feel inside? And the answer has profound implications for us. It is that the emptiness we feel inside is desire and nothing else! So, whilst desire makes it feel as though there is a place inside of us that can be filled up, this is not the case. Our emptiness, our wanting *is* desire. There is no container inside of us, there is no bucket, there is *only* desire.

We have now come to the central part of our understanding which is directly linked to the previous chapters. By saying that there is no place inside us to receive and contain the gains of desire, we are also saying something fundamental about our illusory experience of self. We discover again that when we get to the heart of our desiring self we cannot find a self that can be satisfied. All we find is a process of desire. And this is the point. We are filled with infinite desire because there is no entity to receive, no recipient to take in the products of desire. Because there is no entity of self, no *I* or me, it follows that there is no consumer, no shopper to be satisfied. In other words *there is no desirer, there is only desire.* When I talked before about the illusion of self being just a tension within us, well part of this tension is the process of desire.

From this point of understanding we can see the futility of trying to satisfy our desires with any hope of fulfilment. We are not capable of being satisfied because there is no one to *be* satisfied. We are not a vessel, there is no vessel. Rather, the emptiness we experience is a process of desire that is a central component of our illusory experience of self. In other words, we are the emptiness, the desiring, that needs to go here and there to find fulfilment. Not realising that the real nature of our permanent and separate self is *process*, and a major component of this process is desire, we go out and try to fill ourselves. But everywhere we go and in everything we do, we always bring our empty desiring-self with us. We are empty in one place and we see fullness in another, so we move our empty desiring I-self over to it and find that everywhere else is full of filling, but we are still empty. It is as though we are a bottomless hole in the ground and we travel the world to try and fill ourselves. We go to the movies and the emptiness sits down to take in the pleasures of the film. We buy a car and the emptiness sits down in the front seat and drives off. We go on holiday and the emptiness lies on the beach or tries to take in a beautiful view.

In our desire for fulfilment, we have tried to extract from life what we want. We have attacked life from the outside as though it is our opponent. We have tried to grab and take from it in our effort to consume and add it to ourselves. We have, as Alan Watts expressed it, approached life as though it was *a pie or a barrel of beer.*

The realisation of fulfilment

I trust that what has been said up to now makes sense to you and is sufficiently logical. But there is more: the purpose and impact of these words can bring you much further. If these understandings strike deeply it can move you from understanding to a revelation that can bring an experience of the Tao, a moment of *satori*. When we deeply appreciate the futile and detrimental effects of using desire as a guide to finding the fulfilment that we seek, when we realise this truth with a total seeing, then in an instant our desiring can momentarily switch off. We experience as a fact that we are not empty on the inside. We experience, not as an idea but as a reality, that *we are already full to the brim.*

The fullness that we discover is the result of our

having momentarily broken free from the clutches of our desiring self. When it is seen that desire has no foundation or usefulness, no aim or function other than its own perpetuation, when it is seen that desire is redundant and of no use in our efforts to find fulfilment, then this basic process of self switches off: *we* switch off. We find that our awareness is free of the limits of our desiring self and we experience the peace of a perfect and complete contentment.

Applying the understanding

Now, an immediate breakthrough moment might be nice but it is not necessary. Such a deep seeing through the deception of desire is something that often needs time to percolate into your day to day awareness. Over time the realisation of what is being said can change your relationship with desire. When you feel yourself desiring something, no matter what it is, ask yourself, what is your purpose, what is your motive in satisfying this particular desire? You can, of course, still choose to fulfill that particular desire—but now with a different awareness.

Remind yourself that your desiring is a process that has nothing to do with fulfilment. Desire has nothing to do whatsoever with what you need to find peace within. Need has only brought you more need. Desire can only take you away from getting what you really want. Your efforts to find peace and fulfilment by following desire have been profoundly counterproductive. You have only been maintaining your emptiness and desiring by always seeking outward and away from the place within yourself where there is already a perfectly complete contentment and peace. At the source of your desire, at the source of your emptiness, there already is fulfilment. There is a perfect peace within you and it is your very desire for it that is taking you away from finding it.

You can find this place by seeing through the assumption again and again that you need anything to be happy. You already have what you need to be fulfilled and thinking you need something to be fulfilled is an illusion created by desire.

A story from *The Lotus Sutra* tells of two friends, one rich and the other poor. One day the rich friend was departing on a journey and, feeling sorry for his comrade, he slipped a valuable diamond into his pocket while he was sleeping. The poor man, not knowing he now possessed this great treasure, continued to live a life of poverty. It wasn't until many years later that the two friends met again and the rich man was surprised to find his friend still begging for food. He told him about the jewel and the poor man felt in his pocket and found the diamond.

We too, like the poor man, spend our lives longing and seeking for what it is that we think we need to find fulfilment. And we spend a lifetime doing this without realising that what we seek is already in our possession.

The Tao that desire cannot find

Eastern mysticism has been accused of making our mouths water for enlightenment, whilst at the same time telling us that it is our very wanting it that is preventing our getting it. Now that we know of the Tao it is certainly something else to desire. But here we can come to understand that it is just another thing we desire and as regards our process of desiring it is no more significant than our desire for a biscuit with a cup of tea. It is all the same thing:

The path of material enjoyment is seen to be parallel to the path of search after spiritual joys.

Robert Linssen, *Living Zen*

We can desire all we like and we can desire not to desire all we like. The process of desiring is always in the way and we cannot switch it off. But we can come to see through it even while we are trapped in it; in our search for the Tao we have the freedom of not having to prioritise our desires. Wherever desire takes us in our search for inner peace is the wrong direction, and the moment we think: *Right, so it's the other direction we need to go!* Again we are desiring to be out of there and in a different there instead, and so we go the wrong way again and again.

We find that, having nowhere to turn we are brought back to point zero.

Chapter 6
The self that can't stop doing

IT IS A PERFECT FOLLOW-UP TO OUR CHAPTER ON DESIRE to talk about our *doing* drive. Desiring and doing are inextricably linked for the simple reason that when we desire something, we usually move to the thought: *What can I do to get it?* The want of desire is followed by the urge to do. Both our desiring and our drive to do are central processes of our illusory self and both act as a force within us that orientates us to always seek out and away from where the Tao is to be found.

Identifying doing

When we talk about our drive to be doing I am referring to an inner state that is with us so much of the time that we hardly notice it. This inner state is our inner restlessness. It is our almost constant feeling that we should be busy doing something. It could be described as an inner push or urging that makes it feel as though our lives are in some way being shoved from behind. It's easy to identify this inner restless feeling within ourselves. If we sit in a chair in the middle of a room, we can feel our urge to do something, to be occupied in some way, rising from within. We feel that we should be on the go, moving on, getting on, moving forward.

There is also sometimes a sense of urgency to our doing. We are in a rush to do, to be busy and active. It is as though if we are not busy doing then our existence won't be worthwhile, that if we don't engage in doing we will stagnate—we will be wasting time, left behind, we will miss out. And so we busy ourselves to keep up with a busy life that rushes by.

This inner restless state seems to be a basic fact of our existence and there seems to be no apparent reason for it. It is a strong human characteristic and we can see this if we compare ourselves to the domestic cat, for example. They can laze around all day. As we busy ourselves tending to the garden on a sunny day there is the cat stretched out with paws extended midair. The cat can spend half an afternoon deciding if it wants to jump up onto a wall or not. Animals, apart from attending to their basic needs, seem to feel the 'urge to do' less, but we humans are usually busy being busy.

In our daily lives we have to get a lot of things done, but no matter how many things we get done, even though we may get a break from it, our doing drive with its feeling of inner restlessness soon returns. So again, just as with desire, we are not talking about all the things our doing needs to get done, we are talking about the drive, the push that always accompanies our doing. If it was not for our feeling of inner restlessness we could still get the same things done, but without this feeling of being pushed from behind. We could experience a more peaceful doing.

If we think about our doing drive more deeply it seems that it is accompanied by a vague hope or expectation that our doing is going to bring us to some place, or to get us somewhere in some way. It is almost a sense that if we do enough that at some point we will arrive at a place where everything will be done! It seems that, like desire, we hold a subtle belief that through our doing we can catch up on our inner urging where our inner restlessness can be replaced by a sense of completeness and contentment.

However, rather than getting closer to a place where we have caught up on our inner urging, our doing has not quelled our inner restlessness at all. Our sense of busyness has not decreased. So much of the time we feel rushed to the point that we can even feel guilty when we give ourselves time to relax doing nothing. Soon we feel we must get up and get going again. It seems that there is no connection between our restless doing and getting things done. We are left feeling restless regardless.

Doing is a dynamic of our restless self

The reason we are stuck with this feeling of inner restlessness is not because we have so many things to do. We have a sense of inner restlessness because it is concomitant with having an experience of self. Our endless desiring and our endless doing are basic processes that form part of our experience of self. Our sense of self is restless because we experience ourselves as being still and permanent and separate from a life that is flowing, moving and changing around us. Attempting to maintain our separate identity we are filled with inner restlessness that keeps us busy doing, independent of life's own doing. We feel a restless urge to keep up, to keep busy otherwise we will in some way be left behind.

The result of this is that we must live with the strain of trying to maintain a doing that is outside the natural harmony, movement and flow of life. We cannot just go with the flow, we can't relax into life's own doing. And of course our restless doing is a process without an end. As it is fundamental and inseparable from our experience of self it will exist as long as our illusory identity of self exists.

There are times when we do experience a relaxing of the doing drive. We can be at peace when we have done lots of things and we take a break, either to sit down and relax or when we take a holiday. We experience some peace as we feel there is permission to relax. Our illusory self lessens its grip as our doing drive diminishes for a while.

The doing that keeps us away from the Tao

We are so used to being pushed around by this inner

THE SELF THAT CAN'T STOP DOING

urging that when we search for real happiness, inner peace, spiritual fulfilment we go about it in the same way. And as you picked up this book it was probably with the thought of: *What do I need to do to find the inner peace of the Tao?* And yes, it is helpful to read books such as this one and you can do lots of other things. But what you are being told here—and this is the value of doing the reading of books such as this one—is that thinking you need to *do* anything to discover the Tao will only take you further away:

> *It is only when you seek it that you lose it.*
> *You cannot take hold of it, nor can you get rid*
> *of it. While you can do neither, it goes on its*
> *own way. You remain silent and it speaks; you*
> *speak and it is silent.*
>
> Lao Tzu, *Tao Te Ching*

And your first thought might be: *Come on now! What then do I do—do nothing? Nothing won't get me anywhere!* And you would be right. But what you need to *do* is to realise that the doing drive, like desiring, is redundant and without foundation in your search for the Tao. When it comes to knowing the Tao your inner urging is without basis. There is *nothing* you need to do to discover the peace that lies within. It is our belief that we have to *do* something to find peace and fulfilment that prevents our discovering it! In our search for happiness and fulfilment we have, as with our desiring, been using our inner urging as a signpost to finding it. This inner signpost has been pointing us in the wrong direction all this time. It has kept us oriented and focused on the wrong place. Our doing drive is a process of the self and self can never know the Tao.

The reason you don't have to do anything to know the Tao is because, when it comes to knowing the Tao, everything is already done. You do not have to do a single thing. Your work is done, complete, you are off the hook, you are finished, you can breathe a great big sigh of relief. The inner peace that you seek is already inside you, it is just blocked by your doing, desiring self. When it comes to knowing the Tao you are redundant. There is no entity of *you*, of I-self, moving around doing things, no one who is busy.

Applying the understanding

The question of our doing something in the search for enlightenment is central to Taoist philosophy. Lao Tzu, in the *Tao Te Ching* speaks of *wu-wei* which means *non-doing*. So how do we *do* that? How can we do non-doing? Well we can't! We are trapped in the tension of our illusory doing self. However, when we think: *How can I come to know the Tao?* what we can do is to remind ourselves that there is nothing we need to do, all is already done:

> *Less and less do you need to force things,*
> *until finally you arrive at non-action.*
> *When nothing is done,*

THE SELF THAT CAN'T STOP DOING

nothing is left undone.

Lao Tzu, *Tao Te Ching*

When you feel the *doing* urge rise up within you remind yourself that this is the desiring, doing urge that is actually preventing you from finding the Tao. In your search for the Tao this urge is redundant, it is fooling you, it can only bring you in the wrong direction. And if you experience a moment of realising this deeply then you may experience that:

Sitting quietly, doing nothing,
Spring comes, and the grass grows by itself.

R.H. Blyth, *Haiku*

I could just leave these two beautiful lines out there and let them speak for themselves because if they connect, then they need no explanation. But if they don't connect, what is being said is that life and living have their own momentum and do not need the interference of self. Without the I-self our own living joins the natural harmony of this great movement.

We can apply the understanding to our daily activities, not just in relation to the Tao. As you feel the inner urge to do, the rush to do loads of stuff, just remind yourself that all your doings are not going to bring you inner peace. The inner urging, as with desire, is covering over the inner peace that is already within. Then you can go about doing what needs doing. But, as with desire, if there a deep seeing that the doing drive is redundant, then we might discover what Tibetan monks have found.

In isolated hermitages where it is said they can live on a diet of moonbeams and dew,[3] they have discovered the Tao in their ordinary daily activities:

How wondrous, how miraculous this—
I draw water and I carry fuel!
In spring, the flowers, and in autumn the moon,
In summer a refreshing breeze, and in winter the snow.
What else do I have need for. [4]

Chapter 7
The self that cannot know the present moment

JUST AS OUR EXPLORATION OF *DOING* PERFECTLY followed our exploration of *desire*, so now we follow those with an exploration of *time*. Doing and desire are both driven by an aspect of time: the future.

Our relationship with time, just as with our doing and our desiring, is wholly self-driven. The result is that we are constantly misled as to where the Tao—inner peace—is to be found. Our illusory experience of self causes us to live under a powerful misconception about the nature of time. In this chapter we will find that by coming to a new understanding of our relationship with time, we can discover the special place in time wherein lies the timeless Tao.

The missing aspect of time

Consider how we usually experience time. In general we think of time as time passing. We think of yesterday or last year and get a sense of the days or years that have gone by. And if we think of tomorrow or the years ahead we have a sense of the time that is coming. When the afternoon comes it can feel as though the morning has flown by. When we look at a clock on a wall it seems as though we can actually see time passing. The seconds and minutes go by as the hands of the clock go round. This general experience of time makes sense to us, it fits our world view, and we operate according to it.

But, when we explore our experience of time a little more deeply, it seems that something is not quite right. It seems that there is a missing aspect to our experience of time. What is missing is the *now*, the present moment. An understanding of the now provides one of the most exciting insights of where the Tao can be found.

Consider for a moment where your experience of the now occurs in time. Your answer may be that the now is the point at which you experience the flow of time, that it is the point at which the future arrives and then becomes the past. So we could take, for example, our looking forward to doing something like seeing a movie at some time in the future. Day by day this future expectation draws nearer and when the time comes to see the movie it becomes the now. As we watch the movie it moves from a future expectation to a present experience and then into the past.

However, if we take a closer look at how we experience the present there is something puzzling. For where exactly is the now in our present

THE SELF THAT CANNOT KNOW THE PRESENT MOMENT

experiencing? Where is the point at which the future becomes the past? The moment we try and consider this we find that the moment is gone before it can be grasped. We scarcely have time to notice what the present moment brings before it is gone and gone and gone. It goes by so fast that we can hardly even tell if we have experienced it! It appears that we can only be aware of it by remembering it once it has moved into the past.

And this is the missing aspect of our experience of time. Our experience of the present moment is forever elusive. It seems that we can never be aware of the present moment but only of the past or the future. When we think about the past it stretches back a long way, back further than we can imagine. And when we think about the future it seems to have an infinite duration. But when we think about the present we cannot get a sense of it having any duration at all. Our experience of time seems to be made up of all past and all future with nothing inbetween.

The puzzling thing about our situation is that we are always in the present. Where else can we be? Whilst we feel that the present moment has no duration at all it is the only aspect of time that we are actually in! So it seems a contradiction that the aspect of time that we can relate to, the past and the future, is the aspect of time that we can never actually be in at all. We can conclude that the past doesn't actually exist because it is gone and the future does not exist because it has not come yet. The present is all that actually exists. So why don't we feel as though we experience it?

The present moment that self cannot know

The reason for our feeling as though we do not experience the present moment is connected with our illusory experience of self. Having an identity of self means that we feel ourselves to be separate from all our experience, including the flow of time. A good way of examining our relationship with time, from our dual perspective (*I* on the one hand and *time passing* on the other), is by thinking of a river as representing the flow of time.

Imagine that you are standing on the bank of this river and watching it flow by. We could say that upstream is the future time coming towards us. The place where the water passes us as we stand on the riverbank is the present moment and the water that moves on downstream is the past.

From this perspective it is easy to regard the water that has flowed by as being the past and the water that has yet to pass, as being the future. But when we consider the present aspect of this river of time we find that we run into the same difficulty. For as we go over to the river of time and point to the present moment in our experience we find that it is moving. If we put our hand into the water we find that the present is rushing through our fingers and, the moment we conceive of it, it is gone... and

THE SELF THAT CANNOT KNOW THE PRESENT MOMENT

gone… and gone. And this is why we feel that our experience of time has something missing. It is no wonder then that we have no sense of the present when it is a flowing, moving thing that we experience as passing us by.

We cannot experience the moving present because in our illusion of separateness we are stationary, and not involved in its passing. We can only observe time from our stationary position on the riverbank. We cannot go with its flowing. The only aspect of time that we can relate to is that aspect of time that we can make still. We can know the past because we can fix and make it still by thinking about memories and we can think about and make still the future through our imagining.

And this is the problem we face when we try to heed the often-heard advice to 'live in the present', 'savour the moment', 'live for the now'. In attempting to do this we are attempting the impossible: we cannot be aware of the present moment because it is always moving and passing us by. As soon as we focus on a present experience it has become the past. In our efforts to live in the present we find ourselves taking snapshots of experience, trying to freeze-frame them for an instant before moving onto the next one. Our attempted vigilance becomes constrictive rather than freeing. Experiencing ourselves as separate, permanent and still means that the present must always be a missing aspect of our experience of time.

The illusion of time passing

To know something of the Tao that is hidden by time, we can become aware of the illusion that underpins the way we experience time. We can consider this illusion by returning to our standpoint on the riverbank from where we observe the river of time flowing by.

It is this imaginary standpoint that forms the basis of a powerful misconception that prevents us from knowing the Tao. This standpoint is illusory and is created by our illusory experience of I-self. There is *no* entity of self that is separate from the river of time. There is no one to stand on the riverbank to watch time flowing by. Whilst our illusory experience of self makes it feel as though we are outside and separate from times passing, we are not. We are *in* the river of time and we flow with it. The water that is passing by in the present moment has you in it. We are inseparable from its movement. Time does not go by as the second hand of the clock goes by: whilst we feel that we can watch time go by, the movement of the hands of the clock is not the movement of time passing. The hands move just as the branch of a tree moves. You cannot watch time go by—because you go by with it.

The eternal now

We can begin to see where the present moment is; we have got a hint of it. For if we are moving with the time passing aren't we also *in* the present moment? As we flow along *in* the river of time we are always in the present moment. But, if I were to say: *Jump into the river of time!* this would be the central misunderstanding. There is no-one to jump in. We are in a present moment that does not pass us by because there is no one, no I-self, for it to pass.

This is why we can say that time itself is illusory. If there is no such thing as time passing us by, because there is no one for it to pass, it follows that, from our perspective, there is no such thing as a future that flows into the past. There is of course a past as far as history and previous events are concerned and there is also a future in that life will go on but as far as we are concerned, this all occurs in the present.

When we think about the past or the future, we are not standing outside time thinking about time that has passed us by. A memory of the past is not the past. It is a new experience, happening in the present. A memory is a present experience in the same way as eating a sandwich is a present experience. So too, our thoughts about the future are not the future. Again, thoughts of the future are a new experience occurring in the present. Thoughts of past or future are occurring in the present and it is the same present experience of what is right now before your eyes.

Whether we are thinking about the past or the future, the experience of thinking is always a present one. It is completely new and has no connection with a time that has passed or is to come. For us there is no past or future, there is only the memory of past events or thoughts of future events that happen in our present awareness that is *now*. There is no future that is 'coming' and there is no past that has 'gone' because the idea of a *you* towards whom a future is coming, or a past that has gone by, are illusory:

> *Time is of your own making*
> *Its clock ticks in your head.*
> *The moment you stop thought*
> *Time too stops dead.*

Angelus Silesius, *The Cherubinic Wanderer*

When we talk about the illusion of time we are saying that there only is this present moment. And it is a present without a past or a future. There only is this *now* that is without a beginning or an ending. Our whole lives will be spent in this *now*! From our position of duality our consideration of a *now* that is eternal seems contradictory. But when we experience the Tao we see that the past shares the very same *now* that we are currently in.

The future is not present moments stretching ahead, it is an ever-expanding present moment.

> *The morning glory which blooms for an hour*
> *Differs not at heart from the giant pine,*
> *Which lives for a thousand years.*

Alan Watts, *The Way of Zen*

THE SELF THAT CANNOT KNOW THE PRESENT MOMENT

As we are trapped in the illusion of self, we experience time as rushing by and as we grow older and accumulate more memories, it appears to go by faster and faster. No wonder we can't find peace, for life keeps coming at us. Now imagine again you are standing on the riverbank of time and you watch the water flow by. This time put your hand into the water and experience the river of time running through your fingers. Now imagine your hand could experience the present moment, moving in perfect flow with the current. As you then immerse yourself in the river and experience yourself flowing in perfect synchrony with the water, there is no current. You are flowing as life is flowing. There is only profound peace and stillness. As 'you' are swept away we see that:

> *"Oh, Wondrous", exclaimed the master,*
> *"I am on the bridge, and lo,*
> *it is not the river that is flowing,*
> *but the bridge which is moving up stream!"*

Robert Linssen, *Living Zen*

Now is the only moment

We can use our new understanding of time to find a way to know the Tao by considering how we have always searched for it where it is not. Our search, our hope and our expectation of attaining happiness, inner peace, enlightenment are always based on finding it in a future time. And every time we search for the Tao where it is not, we are reinforcing the erroneous idea that there is a self that is separate from time's passing. The result is that we are always oriented away from what is *now*. And the connection with our desiring and our doing is clear here. These processes have been reinforcing our seeking the Tao in a future time. Our doing and desiring is always about arranging a future time to get what is only available to us *now*.

We can become aware of the power of the present moment by considering that any thoughts of *becoming* enlightened immediately bring us away from where enlightenment, the Tao, is to be found. We cannot become enlightened because there is no future that is coming to us.

The remarkable and exciting fact about what is being said here is that enlightenment, perfect happiness is available to us at this very moment. Right here where we are now. And we have missed this because our lives have been entirely future oriented. We have always postponed happiness. The very moment we are in offers perfect fulfilment. We have looked forward to what the future may bring and all the time we have been oriented away from discovering what is available to us right *now*.

That we truly don't have to go anywhere or be anybody in some future time, is the ultimate freedom. And this is the real meaning of present-moment living. Present-moment living means to realise that there is no need to concentrate on the present moment because now is the only moment there is. To try and focus our attention on it is to suggest that the moment we were just in was somehow not a present one. Again, thinking about the future or the past is a present moment experience. It is not possible for us to be aware of any other moment other than what is *now*. And so, to try and concentrate on the now is to suggest we have been somewhere else, by trying to live in the present we have been trying to somehow double up on where we already are. The moment you are in now is the only place you can and should be. So rather than trying to be aware of the present we need to realise that it is not possible to be aware of anything else. There are no other moments.

Wherefore the absolute tranquility of this present moment,
Though it is at this moment there is no limit to this moment,
and herein is eternal delight.

Alan Watts, *The Way of Zen*

Experiencing deepening moments

As we are trapped in the illusion of self, at our present level of consciousness, we might find that we are trying to force ourselves to live in the *now*. We find that, as we want to gain the hidden riches of the present moment, it has already become a future goal and we find ourselves thinking: *What can I do to get it, to achieve this living in the now?* We cannot avoid this for this is how we are. Now that we are aware of this we are more likely to experience deepening moments where we quietly remind ourselves that, whether we realise it or not, we are already in the *now*. There is nothing that needs to be done to be in the *now*. When it comes to finding enlightenment or inner peace, knowing the Tao, there is nothing in the future for us.

You are right where you should be. Take a rest from your desiring and doing.

You already have it!

Chapter 8
The path to enlightenment

DID DESIRE TRY AND GET YOU TO SKIP TO THIS chapter? *The path to enlightenment*, the ultimate goal of spiritual seekers! Is there such a path? Getting straight to it, and without equivocation… *Yes*, there is a path to enlightenment. However, and you may be half expecting this, it is not a path upon which *you* can walk. Again: *the path there is but none who travel it*.

This may already be clear from the previous pages, for if the self is an illusion, then there is no psychological identity of self to walk a path, there is no one who can be on a path. In a sense your body can, your conscious awareness can, but not a you, not your I-self, for you are a mirage, a puff of smoke. Should *you* try and walk a path towards the Tao, then you will find:

If you move towards it, it moves away.[5]

So how do we get around this, if we involve our I-self we are always going in the wrong direction.

Another way of expressing our predicament is to say that the obstacle is the path and the goal is in the opposite direction to which you seek. But we have to do something for otherwise we will continue to be under the spell of our illusory self. We have the words from a Zenrin poem:

> *You cannot get it by taking thought,*
> *you cannot seek it by not taking thought.*

Alan Watts, *The Way of Zen*

The answer is that we *can* seek enlightenment through the method of direct pointing. The reason we can use this method is because direct pointing is only about pointing at the redundancy of you, at the futility of you, at the obstacle of you in the search for enlightenment. In your search, direct pointing keeps bringing *you* back to point zero.

We have already been using this method. For example, you have read statements such as:

> *What is blocking the Tao so effectively from your view is you, the very you who is wondering what this means.*
>
> *You are in the way of experiencing a deep peace that lies within.*
>
> *There is no connection between the you who was reading this a moment ago and the you who is reading it now.*

You are filled with infinite desire because there is no entity to receive, no recipient to take in the products of desire.

There is nothing you need to do to find enlightenment, all is already done.

You cannot become enlightened because there is no future that is coming to you.

This is all direct pointing.

There are many paths that you can travel to, or towards, enlightenment (I say *you* because it will be the illusory identity of the I-self starting out on the journey). We have looked at some of them previously, particularly the practice of meditation. Whatever the practice of your choice, you may find that coming to an understanding of the illusion of self, through the method of direct pointing, will help in your practice.

Zen and direct pointing

We mentioned before that direct pointing is a favoured method of Zen, in addition to meditation and some other practices. It is used to point directly at the nature of the mind, the illusion of self. There are many Eastern spiritual texts with poems and stories full of direct pointing.

Zen is well known for its use of the *koan* as a method of direct pointing. Here the student is given a paradoxical statement to solve—a statement that is impossible to solve. The student is instructed to dwell on the problem until their mind gives up, with the hope that they might experience a breakthrough moment and experience *satori*. Two well-known koans are: *What is the sound of one hand clapping?* and *What was your original face before you were born?* Zen monks might meditate on these koans for many years as a method of seeking enlightenment. Yes, impressive dedication and resilience!

In the koan method the aim is to encourage a moment of transcendence where the I-self gives up and lets go, as a result of experiencing its own redundancy in solving the problem. It lets go because it has nothing to cling on to. In a similar way direct pointing confronts the self with its own redundancy, its uselessness, in seeking enlightenment.

Bodhidharma

Direct pointing is originally attributable to a semi-legendary Buddhist monk called Bodhidharma. He is credited with bringing Zen to China, in the 5th or 6th century. I am giving Bodhidharma a separate heading here because I think he deserves it! He may have had a strong influence on the development of Zen as a pure, direct and genuine form of seeking.

There are many stories about Bodhidharma. Whether they are true or mythical we do not know. He is sometimes referred to as the 'blue eyed barbarian' and one story tells us that he travelled to a Shaolin monastery but was refused entry. Instead of leaving the area he moved to a nearby cave where he is said to have faced a wall for nine years, not speaking for the entire time. He was then admitted to the Shaolin monastery, a good result but a long wait!

As regards Bodhidharma's method of direct pointing there is a lovely example of it in a story told by Dwight Goddard in *A Buddhist Bible:*

> Emperor Wu of Liang was very favourably inclined towards Buddhism; he founded temples, supported monks, and translated scriptures, but when he asked Bodhidharma during an interview what credit he had earned, the gruff old monk replied, "None whatever, your majesty." To the question, "What is the first principle of the holy doctrine?" Bodhidharma replied, "Vast emptiness, and there is nothing in it to be called 'holy,' Sire."
>
> "Who is it, then, that confronts me?" asked the Emperor.
>
> "I do not know, Your Majesty."

This direct pointing can only help dispel any notions that Emperor Wu might have had about his *self* building up some kind of spiritual credit as a means to enlightenment. This example of direct pointing by Bodhidharma is direct, genuine and also very brave!

In the following two chapters we will be doing some direct pointing to bring you to the limits of your understanding. We will be referring to some of the beautiful and paradoxical Eastern texts, mostly from Zen Buddhism and the *Tao te Ching*. These chapters contain pure Zen, so keep in mind that the writings might make no sense to you or you may have a vague sense that something meaningful is being pointed at. So, if you are confused that is fine, you are being kept on the *path of no path* where it may be discovered that there is no path to travel.

You are right where you should be.

You are simultaneously at the start and the end point of your journey.

Point zero.

Chapter 9
The seeking that takes us away

STRAIGHT AWAY WE HAVE THE DIRECT POINTING OF paradox, the seeking that takes us away. This can only keep us at point zero for where can we go? This is what paradox does. It forces us to face the reality of where we are now, in this place and in this moment. It forces self, *you*, to be redundant—there is no use for you in your spiritual search. This applies to all facets of our seeking to know the Tao.

We have already explored how seeking through desiring, doing or in time can only take us away from where the Tao is to be found:

> *Approach it and there is no beginning;*
> *Follow it and there is no end.*
>
> R.H. Blyth cited by Alan Watts, *The Way of Zen*

There is nothing useful we can do, we are trapped in a dream prison: we are imprisoned in the illusion of self. We stand in the way of ourselves and anything we do to get out of the way will bring us no further. The paradox is that *you* are identical with the problem. The trapper is the trapped, the prisoner is the prison itself!

There is not a doer within us. Within us is a process that is spontaneous and that occurs without any interference whatsoever. When the tension of self is released, we discover that within us there is only stillness, as beautifully conveyed in these Zen poems:

In the dark forest
A berry drops:
The sound of the water.

and:

The skylark:
Its voice alone fell,
Leaving nothing behind.

Alan Watts, *The Way of Zen*

Seeking in time

Consider this Zen account of a conversation between Zen master Ma-tsu and his student Po-chang. They were out for a walk when they saw some wild geese fly by:

"What are they?" asked Ma-tsu.

"They're wild geese", said Po-chang.

"Where are they going?" demanded Ma-tsu.

Po-chang replied, "They've already flown away,"

> *Suddenly Ma-tsu grabbed Po-chang by the nose and twisted it so that he cried out in pain.*
>
> *"How," shouted Ma-tsu, "could they ever have flown away?"*
>
> *This was the moment of Po-chang's awakening.*
>
> Alan Watts, The Way of Zen

Now there might not be anyone to grab your nose in moments such as this but consider what could be wrong with saying that the geese have already flown away? There is nothing wrong with it of course but the enlightened Ma-tsu was trying to confront the student with the paradox of his dual awareness, where the self is experienced as stationary and outside time. For the enlightened Ma-tsu the present moment is not experienced as the future arriving into the present. Rather the present moment is new and original each instant. There is no connection between this moment and the one that comes next or the one that came before because there is no moment that is coming or is going. There is no future moving into the present and there is no present moving into the past. Again, attempting to seek in time brings us right back to point zero.

Seeking what we cannot know through knowledge

In this book I have spoken about coming to know

the Tao. I say to 'know', rather than ' becoming more knowledgeable', because knowing, as we have said before, points to having a profound insight that goes beyond the intellectual level. This insight is more intuitive—you can just *know* something without being able to put it into words. In contrast, gaining knowledge feels more like an activity of the self. When we think that we have knowledge of what the Tao is we, again, are only moving further away from knowing it:

> *Wordiness and intellection*
> *the more with it the further astray we go*
> *Away therefore with wordiness and intellection,*
> *And there is no place where we cannot pass freely.*
>
> Alan Watts, *The Way of Zen*

The problem is that you are the one who becomes further encumbered with whatever knowledge you are accumulating. And immediately you are faced with the problem: the moment you conceptualise the meaning of what is being said here, you have so moved further away from getting it! And as you think about this you have just done it again. And as you contemplate this you have just moved further away, and on this point further away again. And if you think the way is about giving up on knowledge then you have just been led away again. See how you are being kept at point zero!

This account of a conversation between a monk and the Zen master, Hogen, illustrates the point well:

A monk said to Hogen, "When I was studying under Seiko, I got an idea as to the truth of Zen"

"What was your understanding then", asked Hogen.

"When I asked the master who was the Buddha (i.e. what is Reality), he said 'Ping-ting comes for fire'"

"It's a fine answer", said Hogen, "but probably you missed understanding it. Let me see how you take the meaning of it"

"Well" explained the scholar, "Ping-ting is the God of fire. For him to be seeking for fire is like myself, seeking the Buddha. I'm the Buddha already, and no asking is needed."

"There!" exclaimed Hogen. "Just as I thought! You are completely off."

The monk was very offended by this and went off but later came back seeking instruction.

"You ask me," said Hogen
"Who is the Buddha?"
Hogen replied "Ping-ting comes for fire"

Alan Watts, *The Way of Zen*

In answering questions about the nature of Zen or the Tao any answer will do and any answer will not do. Pointing, describing, hinting only engages the self. The self cannot know the Tao. The Tao is only known when there is no interference by the I-self. In our interference we only add momentum to our reaching out. And we have just done so again!

ZEN POINTS TO THE EXTRAORDINARY TAO

> *If you want to see, see directly into it;*
> *but when you try to think about it,*
> *it is altogether missed.*[6]
>
> Anne Bancroft, *Zen: Direct pointing to reality*

And the impossible-seeming paradox is that when you understand, or know, what is being said here you may also be close enough to getting it. In trying to grasp what is being said you flit from one understanding, from one idea, to another. And as you do so you may discover the place where lies the realisation that is beyond your understanding. And to come upon this place you discover the ever-so-subtle space that is to be found at point zero. In trying to understand, you dance around this place, but should you fall in you will find:

> *Make the smallest distinction,*
> *Heaven and earth are set apart.*[7]
>
> *Hsin-Hsin Ming*

But we need to have the words so that we can be brought to point zero. A reminder that: You cannot get it by taking thought, You cannot seek it by not taking thought. But when it is known there are no words:

> *Those who know don't talk,*
> *those who talk don't know.*
>
> Lao Tsu *Tao Te Ching*

Seeking through ideas that always have opposites

Another hindrance to knowing the Tao is an essential property of ideas: every idea has an opposite. We know what an idea is by being able to compare it to something to which it is either similar or different. We know what good is because we can compare it with its opposite—bad. We know what a chair is because it has certain properties that are not exhibited by other objects. Can you think of something that you cannot compare to something else? Even such seemingly all-encompassing words as 'void' can be compared to non-void.

In chapter 1 we considered 'the impossible what' in trying to say what the Tao is. We found that we couldn't begin to describe the Tao because, no matter how inclusive our concept was, it always excluded ourselves. And there is no avoiding this because holding to any concept means that we are aware and therefore outside it.

But the problem also lies in the words themselves that we use to represent the Tao. For words, when they represent concepts, must always exclude (but also infer) their opposite. In trying to describe the unity that is the Tao we can, for example, only consider the concept of everything by being able to compare it with nothing. There is no word that can describe the unity that we call the Tao:

> *It cannot be called void or not void,*
> *Or both or neither;*
> *But in order to point it out,*
> *It is called 'the Void'.*

Alan Watts, *The Way of Zen*

The word Tao represents the unity that is the source of all words:

> *The unnamable is the eternally real.*
> *Naming is the origin*
> *of all particular things.*

Lao Tzu, *Tao Te Ching*

In our quest for what is spiritual we seek to get away from what is not spiritual. In wishing to feel good we try to get away from feeling bad. In seeking the enlightened mind we try to get away from our unenlightened mind. And in pursuing the idea of our goal we cannot get away from its opposite:

> *The perfect Way is without difficulty,*
> *Save that it avoids picking and choosing.*
> *Only when you stop liking and disliking*
> *Will all be clearly understood.*[8]

Hsin-hsin Ming

Seeking to know a movement that cannot be contained in an idea

In trying to know the reality of the Tao, the I-self is trying to form an idea of what is a dynamic, moving and changing reality. But the only ideas that the self can have are static, still and unmoving. They are dead things. They cannot possibly convey a knowing of the actual reality that is the Tao. Instead, they get in the way of a realisation that is only had through direct experience. The self can never have this direct experience because the *I* identity relates only to ideas and concepts that are snapshots of the reality that they represent. We could compare this to our desire to actually experience a beautiful moving seascape when all we have is a photograph.

When we try to know the Tao through an idea, we are trying to fix it as an idea by containing it and making it still. We are trying to know something dynamic when we can only experience the idea that, by its very nature, is static. We might think that we know a river as a moving, changing thing but this is not the case. We can only know frozen snapshots of its existence. It is like a celluloid film strip that gives the impression of movement. When we look closer we see that each frame contains no movement at all.

The great movement that is the Tao can be known only through direct experience. It cannot be known through ideas and concepts in our mind. Ideas cannot contain movement just as a vessel cannot contain the river. The paradox is that in trying to know the Tao through ideas we are looking for wind in a box. The Tao is moving but not moving in relation to anything else:

> *But such a tide as moving, seems to sleep,*
> *Too full for sound or foam.*
>
> Alfred Lord Tennyson, *Crossing the Bar*

Seeking out and away from where it is to be found

In our seeking we are always oriented away from the place where the Tao is to be found! When we consider this, we cannot help ourselves from trying to work out where this place is. And as we do so we are prevented from seeing that the Tao is right here!

> *Like the empty sky it has no boundaries,*
> *Yet it is right in this place, ever profound and clear*
> *[...]*
> *The great gate is wide open to bestow alms,*
> *And no crowd is blocking the way.*
>
> Alan Watts, *The Way of Zen*

You do not have to go anywhere or look anywhere to find it. It is so close that *you* keep missing it. There is no distance between you and the Tao whatsoever:

THE SEEKING THAT TAKES US AWAY

Without opening your door,
you can open your heart to the world.
Without looking out of your window,
you can see the essence of the Tao.

Lao Tzu, *Tao Te Ching*

Chapter 10
Seeking what we already have

WE HAVE ARRIVED AT WHAT, IN OUR SEARCH FOR enlightenment, is perhaps the greatest paradox of all. We already are enlightened! Our goal has been reached. We already have what we are searching for.

The paradox that we already are enlightened

That we already have what we are searching for brings us back to point zero in a striking way. Again, in our seeking, we are like the beggar who didn't know the diamond was in his pocket all along. The riches were already within, whilst his seeking and his desire kept him away from this realisation.

It's so clear that it takes long to see
You must know that the fire which you are seeking
Is the fire in your lantern
And that your rice has been cooked from the very beginning. [9]

Hajime Nakamura

When the illusion of self is removed from our awareness it is seen that we are already there, we have already arrived, and that we were never anywhere else in the first place.

> *Not knowing how near the Truth is*
> *People seek it far away—what a pity.*
> *They are like him, who in the midst of water,*
> *Cries in thirst so imploringly.*
>
> Alan Watts, *The Spirit of Zen*

Unclean words

It is because we already have what we seek that we must consider words such as 'enlightenment' and 'nirvana' as words of deceit. They point the self away from what already *is*. They can be called 'unclean words' because they contaminate our thinking. Of all the words in our seeking vocabulary they are the ones that ring most hollow. For what other words can offer so much and yet give so little to self. As far as the self—the *I*—is concerned, these words are entirely devoid of meaning.

Not only are these words 'unclean', they are offensive; they embody a confidence trick—a con. They suggest that there is some entity that can achieve enlightenment. There is no realisation, no liberation, no Buddhahood to be achieved because there is no one to achieve it. A Zen master put it this way:

Bodhi and Nirvana are like hitching posts for a donkey

Alan Watts, *The Way of Zen*

It is for this reason that students of Zen can be told: *Wash out your mouth every time you say, Buddha!* Or when asking questions such as: *What is Buddha?* the irreverent answers can be: *It is dried dung,* or *the head of a dead cat.*

The rightful protest

At this stage many of us may raise a (reasonable) protest along these lines:

> *This is all very well but it makes no difference to me whether I already am enlightened or not, what matters to me is that I am not feeling it.*
>
> *I am not feeling the inner peace that I seek.*
>
> *And I know, at least in theory, that my identity of self is illusory, but again I'm not feeling it.*
>
> *What I am reading here is not useful!*

If this is where you are, that *is* perfectly reasonable. This is the nature of paradox, it is only useful if it produces a spark or a glimpse of knowing.

But consider this—and it is a strikingly subtle point: whether or not you get this is irrelevant, *you* are redundant. Your true nature is already enlightened and the fact that your identity is caught up with the tension of self is of no relevance. The tension of self with which you identify is an illusion. It is redundant and of no importance whatsoever. The illusion of self has no business wondering about how to become enlightened, for the identity of self is not real and has no basis.

The Tao is so close

If the tension of *you* releases for just a moment and you see it, you will also see just how close it has been all the time. There is just a split hair's difference between seeing it and not seeing it. The Tao is so close that in a sense it is no different to what we are seeing right now. That we are already there means we are already seeing it. And here, again you raise a (reasonable) protest:

But I still don't see it!

But your not seeing it *is it*.

What you are looking for is no different to what you are seeing right now!

*I went there and came back; it was nothing special;
Mount Ro wreathed in mist; Sekko at high tide.*

R.H. Blyth, *Haiku*

There is nothing special or unexpected about the enlightened state for you discover that it is no different to the awareness that you have right now. But because there is no tension of *you* restricting your awareness of it, it is also wondrous, vast and uncontained—and yet just the same, the 'empty and marvellous Tao.'

Giving up seeking what you already have

The self—you and I—can feel disappointed that there is nothing we can *do* to achieve enlightenment. There is no path to follow, no path to work on. We have, in one sense, to give up on it, but the result of such giving up is that we are paradoxically brought more into life in an unexpected and subtle way. If you have been seeking enlightenment for some time you may find that your desire for enlightenment has been your greatest 'being elsewhere' and freedom can come from realising that you can rest in the state of mind you have right now, rather than wishing it was something different.

> *... for you can only be free when even the desire of seeking freedom becomes a harness to you, and when you cease to speak of freedom as a goal and a fulfilment.*
>
> *You shall be free indeed when your days are not without a care nor your nights without a want and a grief,*
>
> *But rather when these things girdle your life and yet you rise above them naked and unbound.*

And how shall you rise beyond your days and nights unless you break the chains which you at the dawn of your understanding have fastened around your noon hour?

In truth that which you call freedom is the strongest of these chains, though its links glitter in the sun and dazzle your eyes.

Kahlil Gibran, *The Prophet*,

Chapter 11
The Tao and our existential questions

We now leave the world of paradox behind and look at how an understanding, a knowing something, of the Tao can give us a different perspective when we consider our big questions about existence. The answers to our age-old questions remain a mystery but an understanding of who is asking can put our questions in a new context.

Is there a God?

We start with the biggest question of all: *Is there a God, a supreme being, a creator?* In the Western world many of us grow up with beliefs about a God and these beliefs largely depend on the culture in which we are raised. We soon find that there are many beliefs that differ from ours, some slightly and some significantly. Before reading this book, you might have explored various beliefs about God and maybe in that exploration you may have come across the religious systems of the East.

The Tao could be considered an Eastern version of God and we have found that it is a God that is discovered through going *in* rather than *out*. Again, the problem with beliefs in a God is that they are ideas being held by an *I*, a *you*, and as a result they take us away from knowing.

Beliefs bring us away from knowing because it is *we* who hold them. We form an idea of our God and struggle to try and come to know this idea in some way. Our efforts are in vain, as the more we try, the more we are constrained and restricted by our idea and so we are all the more caught up in the bondage of self. If we are to discover anything of the Tao we must move to another way of knowing. It is a knowing that is not found through beliefs.

You might expect now that you are going to be told to let go of your beliefs, to free yourself of them, so that you can discover a higher truth. This is a good example of how the search for the Tao can be misunderstood. You do not have to let go of, nor do you have to change, any beliefs you have. Rather what needs to be understood is the futility of searching for a God in this way. If we try to let go of our beliefs then we are just adding something to our to do list and we know where that gets us! Rather, we can just remind ourselves that the self cannot know anything of God; we don't have to believe—or not believe—in anything. We just need to see the wisdom of this. Knowing the Tao is about freedom and no effort is required whatsoever.

When we consider the idea of knowing a God that is not to be known through beliefs, it doesn't mean that we should become non-believers and call ourselves atheists. While atheists and believers seem far apart in their believing, in a way both are in the same place. Atheists are saying that there is no God and believers are saying that there is. Both are labouring under the illusion that the way to know God is through self and through belief. One has found an idea of a God that fits, the other has not. Both are the same distance from finding a God that can be known: to say that we don't believe in the existence of God is just as meaningless as declaring that we do. Both are beliefs about God and they are beliefs that *self* is having.

> *He by whom Brahman is not known, knows It;*
> *He by whom it is known, knows It not.*
> *It is not known by those who know It,*
> *It is known by those who do not know It.*
>
> Kena Upanishad

It is also not the case that this new 'understanding' of what God is, or rather what God is not, is a nihilistic perspective. Not so! The quote above tells us that it is not about believing in nothing. This would be another belief that *you* are having. You may recall that the Buddha taught that the Tao (although he did not call it 'the Tao') is neither void nor non-void; equally it may also be stated that the Tao is neither God nor non-God.

We can see that the concept of the Tao is more

expansive than any idea we are capable of having about God. It is all-inclusive. In considering whether there is a God or not, you are in the dual position of there being a *you* and a God that can be known. The narrow, illusory identity of self is not capable of knowing anything about God. The 'Tao God' is bigger, it is the All. So, going back to the question: *Is there a God?* before we can answer we have to consider whether this is a valid question. And to do that we have to first consider: *Who is asking?* The answer is that there is no-one to do the asking. Again there is no I-self separate from the All so the idea of a separate reference point to ask the question is illusory. Oneness cannot ask about oneness.

What about death?

Questions around our own death are universal. These questions have made our enquiries into whether God exists and whether there is any meaning or purpose to our lives all the more urgent. Our death is the one thing that we know is coming for sure—and we don't like to think about it.

Our pressing question is usually whether the end is really the end or is there an afterlife of some sort. But we are not going to get anywhere by pursuing this question. A more appropriate question that we can ask is: *what do we* mean *by death*? In other words: *who is it that is going to die?* What is it that is going to be ending other than the physical body?

Of course the reason we fear death so much is

because we believe that it is the *me*, the I-self that inhabits this physical body that is going to die. But we now know that this experience of self is illusory. So what does this say about our concerns about death?

The illusory fear of death

Alan Watts likened our wondering what happens to us when we die to wondering what happens to our fist when we open our hand, or where our lap goes when we stand up. When there is no entity of self, no *I* or *you* that exists in the first place, it follows that there is no one to die. What does not exist cannot cease to exist.

We already are at one with the Tao and our own death does not change this. Our energy is identical to the universal energy, we are all the same universal stuff. The only thing that 'dies' on the occasion of our death is the illusion of self. What this means is that what we are really fearing when we fear our own death is the death of a mirage! It is for this reason that the attainment of enlightenment can be regarded as the only real death that can occur in this life. The enlightened life is when we die in every moment. In our quest for enlightenment, we are actually seeking the death of our I-self. It is a powerful irony that we fear our own death and yet we long for the enlightenment that can bring it!

We can use the analogy of the river meeting the sea both to convey the experience of enlightenment and to convey the reality of our own death. Our death can be thought of as being the river of self meeting the sea, the universal Tao. It is a homecoming that brings a return to source, *the source with which we are already at one.*

It can be a liberating experience to come to this more enlightened understanding of death. We can experience the freedom that comes from not being burdened with thoughts that this life is in some way a preparation for what might follow. We are free from the worry of whether we will get to a heaven or who or what we may be reincarnated as. There is only this life and we move from moment to moment without having to carry anything with us. We carry no baggage whatsoever.

What about free will and predestination?

If there is no self within us what then about free will? Do we make decisions, or do they just happen by themselves? And what of the question of predestination—is there an inevitability to our lives? Are our lives going in a predetermined direction no matter what we do?

Looking first at the question of free will and personal responsibility. If you have read the earlier chapters you will have guessed it: there is no entity of self in us to have free will.

So, is there someone in us who decides then? Again, no, there is no separate entity of self who decides. Decisions arise in response to forces acting on individual awareness. We cannot trace back the enormous complexity that produces any decision. We certainly feel as though we decide things but really in the final analysis the experience that *yes I decided such and such*, is just a thought in one stream of consciousness. There is no separate decider in you that evaluates things and then decides. Think of picking up a pen beside you. You can think about it but the actual picking up of it just happens. The idea that there is no decider in us, that it all just happens, sweeps you away. Good!

I like Ramesh Balsekar's words:

Act as if there is free will, knowing that there is no such thing… live as if you are responsible, knowing that the totality is responsible for everything. Events happen, deeds are done, but there is no individual doer thereof. [10]

Ramesh Balsekar, *The Only Way to Live*

What about predestination, the idea that we have no control over events because our lives are determined by fate? Some think that this fate is determined by a God. But is the great movement that we call the Tao set on a predestined course? Is our future set? Future events are the result of an infinite complexity of variables that precede it. At extreme levels of complexity, other factors come into play. Perhaps physics can give us some resolution to this question, with developments in quantum mechanics and assembly theory,[11] which redefines time itself.

For now we have mystery.

What is the meaning or purpose to our life?

We are born onto this planet (without asking), a planet that is a small spinning and orbiting object in one of over 100 billion galaxies. Sometimes we can feel very alone and sometimes we can feel very connected. We are given no manual on living, no explanation about why we are here and what we should be doing now that we are. We get instructions when we buy a toaster, but we get no instructions for living. It would make things so much easier, we think, if we could know what our purpose in life is. It would be comforting, we think, if we could live our lives with the certainty that there is some point to it all.

Sometimes, when we think about it, it can seem that our lives are meaningless and the more we stand back and look at our lives from a wider perspective, the more meaningless our existence can appear. At any one time there are, on this planet we call Earth, about eight billion of us, with half a million being born each day and about 150 thousand dying each day. Imagine you are watching our planet from outer space and you could observe all the little individual lights of births and deaths going on and off. That would be quite a perspective! From a time perspective our current understanding is that the universe is about 13.8 billion years old while homo sapiens has only been here for about 300,000 years. The drama of our individual lives seems petty when we look at things from the larger picture. We can sometimes relate to Macbeth's despair:

> *Life's but a walking shadow, a poor player*
> *That struts and frets his hour upon the stage*
> *And then is heard of no more: it is a tale*
> *Told by an idiot, full of sound and fury,*
> *Signifying nothing.*
>
> Shakespeare, *Macbeth*, Act V Scene 5.

No wonder we want to find a reason for our existence so that we can escape this sense of despair, frustration and nothingness. And while we seek, we believe that our despair is caused by our not being able to find an adequate answer to our questions. And so we search and search.

As we come to an understanding of the Tao we discover that our despair is not caused by the lack of answers, our despair is actually caused by the questions themselves. Our insistence on believing that there should be answers to the questions of meaning and purpose is responsible for the despair and disillusionment that we can experience.

Think on it. Why do we ask such questions? What do we mean by: *What is life for?* Or: *What are we for?* We ask with the presumption that there should be an answer, that there should be purpose and meaning to our lives. But why should there be?

It is because we experience ourselves as being separate from the all-inclusive whole, from the great movement of life, that we think there should be a purpose for us as individuals. Feeling ourselves as separate, we feel there must be a reason for our being here. We feel that life itself is not a good enough reason. We feel that life is somehow the arena within which we can go about and fulfil our own purpose, as though life is secondary or subservient to this goal.

But, as we have discussed, we are not separate from life. Our experience of I-self as separate is an illusion. Our questions of meaning and purpose arise from an illusory experience. If we were to move from our position of duality to non-duality we would find that questions of meaning and purpose do not apply. And it is not the case that life has no meaning. Rather it is that the question itself is seen to be meaningless

The meaning and purpose we overlook

Life *is* inherently purposeful. We overlook this and ask: *What is this inherent purpose?* But there you go again, life *is* purposeful. There is no purpose separate from it. Purposefulness and life are inseparable and when you ask about this you are immediately trying to separate the two. *Our* direction is not separate from *life's* direction. Our lives are not for something that is separate from what life is for and life is not *for* anything. Why should life be *for* something when there is nothing other than what it is! How can life have meaning in relation to itself. Life is inherently purposeful because it is an all-inclusive whole that contains no separation or division. There is nothing outside or other than what it is. It is a unity that is perfectly and completely self-contained. So why then say that there should be any purpose to living other than living? Animals, not being divided within themselves, have no such questions of purpose on their minds. They go about life and know exactly what they should be doing, which is... living.

Our purpose is to do the human thing, to grow and evolve, to live and then to die, nothing more nothing less. An old Zen poem dispenses with any philosophical treatise on the purpose of life when it says:

> *We eat, excrete, sleep and get up;*
> *This is our world.*
> *All we have to do after that—*
> *Is to die.*

Alan Watts, *The Way of Zen*

We may feel a sense of disillusionment to find that this is all that our lives are about, but this is only because we are suffering under the illusion of having a separate and purposeful individual self. When we see that life's purpose is *our* purpose then there need be no sense of disillusionment. Our purpose is identical and in harmony with the great evolving momentum of life. The realisation is ultimately satisfying and reassuring in every way.

The fact that life is not *for* something can relieve us of a stressor in our lives. The understanding that our lives are inherently purposeful, and therefore already purposeful, can turn what may have been despair into relief—in an instant. When we see that our own individual meaning is a redundant question then we can experience the freedom that is here for us. Our independent existence is not *for* anything. We do not have to take our lives seriously. We are free to live for living's sake. We are not burdened by having to fulfil some purpose during our time here. We are relieved of the responsibility to find direction or meaning. We are inseparable from life, we come from stardust. We are part of a great evolving movement that is greater than individual meaning.

What is going on?

What can we say about this great movement that we call *life*? We have found that relativity, astrophysics, cosmology and quantum theory all point towards an underlying unity that is consistent with the words of Lao Tzu:

> *There was something formless and perfect*
> *before the universe was born.*
> *It is serene. Empty.*
> *Solitary. Unchanging.*
> *Infinite. Eternally present.*
> *It is the mother of the universe.*
> *For lack of a better name,*
> *I call it the Tao.*

Lao Tzu, *Tao Te Ching*

We don't know what consciousness is but it appears to be something that is evolving. We moved from early life forms to higher levels of complexity until it seems that consciousness emerged. Matter became conscious. At our current stage of evolution, we have the emergence of self-consciousness. And why should evolution stop here, particularly when we see how our I-centred consciousness has had such an adverse effect on our planetary home? Though we have also achieved great things, it is the case that there are billions of us *I's* going about the planet, a planet of scarce resources, often consuming as much as we can and all of us with competing needs. Surely the high point of evolution is not where we self-destruct. We need to evolve soon, but evolve to what?

Is it the case that the next evolutionary stage is a further consciousness shift, the one that we see in the transcendent state of enlightenment? It is noteworthy that those who appear to have moved to this level of consciousness, or who have had peak states, report experiences of unity with an underlying, connected energy. The word used to describe this state is 'love' though not in the usual sense of the word.

The state is impregnated with an ineffable something which is beyond that which we call love[12]

Will evolution, in time, return to a unity at the

consciousness level? Will this return to unity bring us to know an energy that we call a form of Love. Tao, God, and Love?

Chapter 12
Walking with the Tao

WE ALL WANT TO WALK WITH THE TAO BUT UNLESS we happen to be fully enlightened it will be our self, your self, my self that is traveling the path. We would all like to reach the destination where we realise: *the path there is but none who travel it.* But until we get there, if we get there, however likely or unlikely that might be, it will be *you* who is travelling it.

We have not yet explored the psychological health of the self, because this book is about a transpersonal psychology rather than self-psychology. I work as a psychologist and have been practising psychotherapy for the past 30 years, attending to matters of self. I am smiling here as I write because, on the one hand, I am telling you that I spend my working life dealing with issues of self whilst in this book I am telling you that the self is redundant and of no importance!

This might sound like a contradiction until you realise that the use of the word *self* in this book refers to our I-self, our identity of I-ness, whereas self in self-development psychology and psychotherapy refers to all the things that our I-ness is identified with—all the contents of consciousness. All our thoughts, feelings and emotions are real and important, but what is not real or important is the experience of a separate and permanent *I* experiencing these thoughts, feelings and emotions.

The Tao and the suffering of self

Feelings engage our identity of I-self. Our feelings bloom in the body, they call to us and demand the attention of *I*. The flavour of self can become the flavour of whatever type of body feeling is being experienced. And then these feelings, like clouds in our consciousness, rain down whatever thoughts are associated with them—negative thoughts if they are associated with negative feelings and positive ones if associated with positive feelings.

The extent to which we can use Zen practices and philosophy to deal with these feelings depends on how easily we can access the broader awareness of the Tao and the strength of the particular feelings. We can sometimes experience release through the use of direct pointing by, for example, reminding ourselves of the following:

Although there is the experience of suffering there is no you *who is suffering.*

The you that is suffering is of no importance or consequence whatsoever.

Just wanting not to suffer is desire, desire to be in a different mental state to the one you are in now.

Sometimes this kind of direct pointing can work if we catch the right moment, but often we will find that the particular feeling state we are experiencing will have too strong a grip on self and we will not be able to experience release. It will be the case that we translate the Buddha's maxim in the *Visuddhimagga*: *suffering alone exists, none who suffer* into: *suffering exists and I am suffering.*

The point here is that Eastern spiritual psychology is often neither strong enough, nor appropriate, to deal with problems of the self. This means that we often need to address emotional problems through avenues of self-development psychology or other spiritual psychologies that relate more to self-development. We could say that Eastern spiritual psychologies are about moving beyond *I* whereas self-development psychologies are about helping *I* to function in a healthy way, as free of as much pain and dysfunction as possible.

Do we need a healthy I-centred consciousness to know the Tao? No, not necessarily! People who experience difficulties in their lives are more likely to be drawn to spiritual inquiry and are therefore more likely to develop in that awareness. A number of people who do seem to have moved to the fully enlightened state did so after an intense psychological crisis. It may also be the case that, rather than healthiness of self, it is those who have a philosophical or enquiring mind that may have more potential to know the Tao.

Balanced seeking

While we use the Zen insight method of direct pointing, it is wise to apply it in a relaxed way—we don't have to go on an energetic pursuit of it. Rather we can let Zen drop gently into our lives. You will notice that when you apply paradox there is no strain, there is no task, there is nothing to be done. It is perfect freedom.

If we pursue the Eastern spiritual path too strongly this may have a negative effect on our psychological wellbeing, because, as mentioned earlier, we are on automatic pilot most of the time. We just cannot maintain a constant vigilance where we try and hold onto any particular insights. Unfortunately we soon find that we are lost in our thoughts and internal dramas with all the associated feelings. This is why it's wise to apply insights gently, let them permeate our awareness where they can gradually become the backdrop to our lives.

There are other less intellectual approaches in Eastern philosophies. The main one of course is meditation but you may also like to try some of the movement oriented disciplines such as yoga or Tai

Chi, for example. Such pursuits are useful for self-development and transpersonal development at the same time.

The Tao shines on self

In our spiritual search we are not in an all or nothing situation. It is not the case that either we are experiencing breakthrough moments or that isn't happening and we are left with nothing. If we do come to know something of the Tao for even a moment—if we experience an insight, a glimpse, a brief knowing—it can have a profound impact for the rest of our lives. It is indeed true: *for this one rare event, gladly I would give a thousand coins of gold.*

If we see through the illusion of self for one brief moment, we will not forget what we have experienced. From that moment on we will always know that there is a greater reality to be known beyond the restrictive tension of self. We will also know that there is a deep peace within us that is covered over by the tension of self and that all we need to experience this peace is for this tension to release. Having known the Tao will give us a comfort that we can carry through our lives, a comfort that we will know even in the dark times. Coming back to the analogy of the river and the sea, imagine being a river in life, a river that knew about the sea and had been there.

Knowing the Tao gives us more perspective and understanding of our present conscious condition.

Negotiating our way through life with an I-centred consciousness is challenging and we find ourselves in a world where we are vulnerable, both physically and psychologically. We can come to see that, at any point in time, we are just doing what we can, given the resources, both internal and external, that we have at our disposal. We see that as a result of being trapped in the illusion of self we are also trapped in our personal dramas. We can't prevent the feelings or thoughts that arise within us and we shouldn't feel bad for having them, regardless of their content. Whatever arises in us is not our 'fault'. Whatever is going on is the 'fault' of our present evolved state of consciousness. We use our self-awareness to make the best choices we can and we also use this self-awareness to go easier on ourselves. The more we can allow in the perspective that brings self-acceptance, the more we find that we are walking with the Tao.

Having an I-centred consciousness means that we are always alone in the world. Even though we can have closeness around us, we are alone in our minds. There is no-one who can climb into our mind to be with us. But the Tao can. The Tao can be a presence in our isolation because when we know the Tao we experience connection, the very opposite of isolation. Rather than feeling lonely we can experience how we are a completely integral part of something much greater. For example, we can look at the stars and feel very alone, or we can look at the stars and experience the special place we have in the universe, that we are looking at an extraordinary and beautiful vastness that is our home, and we have a special place in it.

The following Zen poems attempt to communicate something of solitude. The poems can be experienced as being stark, lonely and isolating or they can communicate something magical, joyful and utterly tranquil:

> *Wind subsiding, the flowers still fall;*
> *Bird crying, the mountain silence deepens.*

Alan Watts, *Way of Zen*

and:

> *With the evening breeze*
> *The water laps against*
> *The heron's legs.*

Alan Watts, *Way of Zen*

The I that is we

We all live in the same dream prison and none of us can escape suffering. If you hesitate to believe this, consider how we cannot avoid dealing with loss at some time in our life.

Our own death and the death of others is a given. We all suffer because we live with an I-centred consciousness so we are all equally vulnerable. For all of us exist in a reality that flows by without a care, it seems, for our individual needs. As we saw in the introduction, life can be harsh and some have it easier than others. As we are all in the same boat, on the same often perilous journey, we can wish ourselves and others well and take our luck as it comes.

Knowing the Tao is also the great equaliser. When we know the Tao, we know that the *self*, our sense of *I*-ness, is redundant and of no importance. As a result we can come to feel more neutral about ego things such as status, power or wealth. We can pursue these things and enjoy them, as can others—if we want to. But we can also see that these things are not a measure of self because such things, material or psychological, belong to no one. There is no real, separate and permanent self to scale a measure to. It is because of this that we can find that any feelings we have of superiority or inferiority towards others have nowhere to land. They have nowhere to land because, for example, for my self to feel superior to your self I am making a comparison of my *I* with your *I*. I would be comparing one illusion with the other where both of us are caught in the same spell. We both suffer from the same outrageous confidence trick. If we could see it, we could see that there is no *I* in us and no *I* in the other to be compared.

The concept of the *I* that is *We* also helps when we are feeling troubled by the actions of others. So for example, whether it is our neighbour or some cruel world dictator, we can understand that they too are trapped in the illusion, the spell of *self*. They too have limited resources of whatever cognitive and feeling states happen to be acting in their particular conscious awareness. This is not about trying to forgive or accept what they do. Rather it is about seeing that whatever upset or outrage we feel towards them, can also be directed at the real cause—our present state of I-centred consciousness.

Now that we can think in terms of the '*I* that is *We*' we can embrace the interconnection between idividual consciousness and the greater unity.

Chapter 13
Beware of false paths

Spiritual paths can be treacherous. It is easy to end up on a wrong path, fuel the illusion of self and tie ourselves in knots, so that we experience stress rather than peace. We can talk about a path to enlightenment and it will be a pure path if it leads to the discovery that *there is no-one to be on that path*.

'Spiritual reading' can sometimes be misleading. It is very easy to offer directions for a path towards enlightenment, but often the guidance only engages *self* and does nothing to expose the illusion of *self*. I may have done the same on occasions in this book, it is so easy to say something that misses the point between leaving the printed page and reaching the reader's consciousness. Sometimes, too, when books are written by genuinely, fully enlightened individuals there are occasions when the guidance within comes from their perspective of enlightened awareness that is not always so useful for our 'unenlightened' awareness to follow. It also seems to be the case that for some of these enlightened individuals, their own enlightenment was the result of an intense personal crisis, and not through following any well-known and tested path.

What follows may be useful to keep you off false paths and back on the one...

Caution: adopting an enlightened outlook

This type of advice suggests we should try to see the world from an enlightened perspective, for example: 'give up the ego by accepting all that you are'; 'adopt the mental attitude of non-resistance'; 'say yes to everything whatever it may be'; 'let go and let God'; 'rest in the inner peace that is within you'; 'rest in your natural being'; 'experience our lives as though for the first time'; 'be completely sensitive to each moment'. We may be told that we should 'see' that there is no thinker behind our thoughts and that we should 'see' that we are not separate from our experience. We may be told that all we need to do is to correct our 'vision'. Other advice is to seek enlightenment through living by 'non-action', 'non-making', 'non-doing', 'non-striving' or 'non-busyness'.

Caution: acting like a spiritual person

Sometimes we are encouraged to 'spiritualise ourselves' by acting in the way we think spiritual people act. For example we may be encouraged to 'develop a loving energy' that we should 'let radiate all around us', and people should 'feel our spirituality, compassion and kindness'. The American spiritual teacher, Ram Dass, gave an open account of his pursuit of this false path; he describes how his ordinary self would sit in judgement of his spiritual self. He described his condition as being like 'vertical schizophrenia'.

Now we just cannot possibly do these self-spiritualising activities without becoming unreal and unnatural. Apart from the fact that we are on autopilot most of the time, the states of mind described are a *result* of reaching enlightenment, they are *not* a means to it. If we try and follow this advice we will always be in the position of *who* is going to try not to resist, *who* is going to try to rest in a deep inner peace, *who* is going to be completely sensitive to each moment, *who* is going to try and engage in non-striving, *who* is being spiritual. It will always be the I-self doing these things and all we are doing is perpetuating the illusion of self. Trying to follow such sometimes tantalising advice may only cause frustration, disappointment and sometimes a sense of failure.

> Spiritual advice should always lead us to experience freedom rather than constriction.

Caution: forcing spontaneity

What about trying to be 'spontaneous' in our thoughts and actions? If we could just do things 'without engaging self,' could that be a path to liberation? Again, this is to miss the point. Our experience of a self that does, a doer behind the doing, is an illusion. So who is it then who is not being spontaneous in the first place? Whether we realise it or not, everything about our thoughts and actions is *already spontaneous*. We spontaneously arrive at decisions. We suddenly find that we decide to do something. Certainly, more planning and thought goes into some decisions than others but this planning and considering and weighing up is spontaneous also. There is no one doing it! We cannot but be spontaneous.

Caution: interfering with our thoughts

This type of direction can really tie us in knots. We can be encouraged to keep a constant watchful eye on our thoughts, we should: 'watch our thoughts rather than become them'; 'suppress mental activity'; 'find the space between our thoughts'. We may be told that 'freedom comes when thought ends'. Again, this type of advice is futile. We cannot stop our thoughts and when we try to interfere with them we get thoughts acting on other thoughts and we can end up in a muddle, like the centipede that was walking along fine until someone asked it which leg goes first!

Caution: following the path of acceptance

This advice deserves its own heading as it is often a cause of confusion. When it comes to our spiritual path, we may be offered guidance such as: 'embrace all of our experience'; 'say yes to the universe'; 'adopt an attitude of total acceptance'; 'accept all that is'.

Now to remind you: the advice that we should in some way try and accept all our experience suggests that we are in some way separate from it. Again, there is no separation. It is not the case that the *I* on the one side must merge with an inner reality on the other. There is no *I*.

Consider the path of acceptance if:

But we can use the idea of acceptance if it leads to paradox and brings us back to point zero. We can come to understand that there is no need to try and accept anything. All that needs to be seen is that everything is already accepted. This doesn't leave much for you to do!

Caution: practicing detachment

This is another widely taught false path that we may encounter. When we hear that self is not real we can think: *Yes, this makes sense! I must get rid of self altogether.* We may be tempted to follow guidance such as: 'enlightenment is only possible once you learn to live beyond your personality'; or that 'enlightenment is a state of mind... a genuine and lasting detachment from emotional unhappiness'. And furthermore, we may be told that this detachment is achieved through undeviating concentration on the goal. Now as you may already see, the goal is not to try and get rid of self as self is not real in the first place. It would be like trying to dig up a desert mirage with a spade! And again, who would be doing the digging? You guessed it—you!

Caution: suppressing the self

The same applies to efforts to suppress self. We can come upon guidance that we should practice 'self-restraint, self-purification through willing sacrifices' or that we should 'negate our basic appetites and desires' and only engage in pure living. We mentioned before that the Buddha followed a path of asceticism for a while. It was harmful, both physically and psychologically, and he had to give it up.

Consider Meditation

Meditation is a favoured method of Eastern religions for seeking enlightenment. Many techniques have evolved over the centuries and we looked at some of the different practices earlier. We spoke of Bodhidharma who, as legend has it, meditated facing a wall for nine years and there are many other accounts of monks who would sit in meditation in caves for long periods of time. In some monasteries monks asked to be bricked up in small cells with just a hole in the wall large enough for food to be passed through. This may sound like torture but it must have been worth it for the blissful states they experienced.

But how successful is the practice of meditation in achieving spiritual enlightenment? We should really ask someone like Bodhidharma (or you, yourself, if you are a long term practitioner of meditation). However for the purpose of this book we can explore the following words from a Buddhist text:

Mantras and tantras, meditation and concentration,
They are all a cause of self-deception.
Do not defile in contemplation thought that is pure in its own nature,
But abide in the bliss of yourself and cease those torments.
Whatever you see, that is it,
In front, behind, in all the ten directions.
Even today let your master make an end of delusion!
The nature of the sky is originally clear,
But by gazing and gazing the sight becomes obscured.

Alan Watts, *The Way of Zen*

This brings us back to what has been referred to above when we looked at 'advice to adopt an enlightened outlook'. We would absolutely 'abide in the bliss of ourselves' if we could, in a heartbeat. However such advice also rings true and this book has contained similar commentary. What is being said here is no different to what has been said in chapter 10 'Seeking what we already have'. Doing *anything* to further our enlightenment only moves us further away from getting it. And so 'the nature of the sky is originally clear' because there is nothing within us to change or transform.

Again, the paradox of our situation is that, we say there is nothing to be done but, at the same time, we also have to do *something*, for otherwise we will continue to be under the complete spell of the I-self. We are trapped in our illusory dual consciousness and we are not able to follow the advice to, 'abide in the bliss of ourselves'. Whilst we already are enlightened, we don't *feel* it because we experience our illusory self as being real and we identify with it. Even though 'the sky is originally clear' we do not experience it as such. So we need to 'do' something.

Whatever form of meditation we are practicing we can be mindful that we sit in paradox. We can sit in both the futility of our seeking and also in the necessity of our seeking at the same time. So when we sit in meditation, we find ourselves trying to do so without hope or expectation. And as we twist and turn and try and trick ourselves into thinking this is so, we find that anything we do or try not to do only adds momentum to the self that cannot sit without expectation.

In our struggle we may come to the place where we just sit, in the very place that we already are.

Chapter 14
Peace comes dropping slowly

What should you expect in terms of your own spiritual enlightenment? This is the important question we address at this, our final chapter and this book-journey's end.

Achieving full enlightenment is rare and difficult. It may be why there are so many different Eastern religious systems, schools and sects with the resulting plethora of spiritual practices. This suggests that no particular practice has been the 'right' method.

How far we go on our own spiritual journey depends to what extent we are caught up in the spell of the illusory self—and it seems that we are all different in this respect. If enlightenment is connected to the evolution of consciousness, then the possibilities of enlightenment may depend on your own unique brain physiology as well.

What we are discussing here is *full enlightenment*, a complete and permanent 'passing through'. For many of us I think it may be wiser to think in terms of living a semi-enlightened life. We spoke before of how the Tao can shine on self and perhaps this is a good way to describe what such a semi-enlightened life might be like. Sometimes the sun (the Tao) will shine very brightly on self and we experience freedom, peace and joy in our lives. Sometimes the sun can burn up self and we experience *satori*. At other times the self might be buried under a cloud (especially when pulled into body pain) and we experience little or nothing of the Tao. And sometimes it can be just dark. However, no matter how enveloped in a cloud we might be, we will always know that just above the cloud the Tao will always be there, and it is shining.

As for expectations I came across the words of Hakuin Ekaku. He was born in 1686 and grew up near Mount Fuji in Japan. He became a monk at the age of 16 and later reformed the Rinzai school of Zen. He advocated arduous meditation and *koan* practice'[13] I give you these details to show you how dedicated Hakuin was in the pursuit of enlightenment. As regards his experiences he tells us:

> *Six or seven times I have had the bliss*
> *of passing through,*
> *and times without number the dancing joy.* [14]

C.Humphreys, *A Western Approach to Zen*

How peace might come

As you work with the various insights and understandings in this book, as the tension of self is again and again faced with its own redundancy, you can find that a freeing process takes place. Self becomes lighter and you are more likely to experience *satori*. The understandings begin to become part of a growing wisdom that forms the backdrop against which you live your life. The more you see into your true nature, the more you experience sparks or inklings of knowing, the more you will also begin to experience the peace, connectedness, freedom and deepening moments that knowing the Tao brings. It is true that, as William Butler Yeats describes in his beautiful poem, *The Lake Isle of Innisfree*,[15] this peace does come 'dropping slow'.

Travelling light

Freedom comes slowly too. It comes to us gently as we realise there is nothing we need to do or to have—we already have it. There is nowhere we need to be other than where we are now. We can rest where we are in this very moment. We are free as we realise we are not for something, other than what life is for. We can be as we are. And we can let peace come, we don't have to seek it. In finding our path we find that the ground is truly taken from under us:

> *Above, not a tile to cover the head;*
> *Below, not an inch of ground for the foot.*
>
> R.H. Blyth, *Haiku*

This freedom is absolute, it is in our daily life and can be found at every turn. It is available to us whether we are stuck in a frustrating traffic jam or viewing a beautiful sunset. We can find it in the trip into town just as it is in the meditation retreat. It is also available regardless of our situation in life. It is our birthright. It is here and now in this very moment, instantaneously and immediately.

The miraculous is in the ordinary.

As our knowing deepens we begin to discover what can only be called the *isness* of life. This is the growing sense that we are moving along with life's unhindered momentum. In our flowing, rather than resisting, we experience what are the givens of life. We begin to experience that, despite our opposition and attempt to control the flow of reality, it goes on regardless. The momentum begins to sweep us away as we transcend the constraints of self and begin to experience the Tao. In expressing the Tao we find that all that can be said is that it so perfectly, simply and clearly *is*. There is something else which comes with the experience of *isness*. We experience in an absolute way that everything is okay, that everything is perfectly alright. Nothing can happen to us, for we happen as life happens. We know we are not the river, we are the sea and have always been the sea.

Go easier now, knowing how special you are! We are the result of billions of years of evolution, we have been forged out of the great furnaces of stars. For now we are challenged by the limits of our I-centred consciousness. But we represent so much more for we possess a consciousness that when freed of the tension of self can expand in all directions, with apparently no limits to its expansion.

The universe is in the palm of your hand.

Endnotes and Citations

1. Seppola, E. feeling-it/201309/20-scientific-reasons-to-start-meditating-today. Available from: www.psychologytoday.com/gb/blog/ [online] accessed 24/7/2023.
2. Coxhead, N. (1985) *The Relevance of Bliss.* London: Wildwood House.
3. Macy, J. (2000) in Kaza, S. (ed) *Dharma Rain: Sources of Buddhist Environmentalism.* Boulder: Shambhala Publications.
4. Nakamura, H (1998) *A Comparative History of Ideas.* New Delhi: Motilal Banarsidas
5. Blackstone, J. (2008) *Zen for Beginners.* Newburyport: Red Wheel/Weiser.
6. Bancroft, A. (1979) *Zen: Direct pointing to reality.* London: Thames & Hudson.
7. Osho. (2009). *Hsing Hsing Ming: The Book of Nothing.* New York: Osho Media International.
8. Osho. Ibid.
9. Nakamura, H. Ibid.
10. Balsekar, R. (2013) *The Only Way to Live.* Mumbai: Yogi Impressions.
11. Walker, S.I. (2023) 2023-04-life-modern-physics-itbut-theory.html. Available from www.phys.org/news/ [online] accessed 24/7/2023.
12. Coxhead, N. Ibid.
13. Waddell, N. (Tr.)(1999) *Wild Ivy: The Spiritual Autobiography of Zen Master Hakuin.* Boston: Shambhala Publications, Inc.

14. Humphreys, C. (1999) *A Western Approach to Zen*. San Raphael: Mandala Books
15. W.B.Yeats: *The Lake Isle of Innisfree*

I will arise and go now, and go to Innisfree,
And a small cabin build there, of clay and wattles made;
Nine bean-rows will I have there, a hive for the honey-bee,
And live alone in the bee-loud glade.

And I shall have some peace there, for peace comes dropping slow,
Dropping from the veils of the morning to where the cricket sings;
There midnight's all a glimmer, and noon a purple glow,
And evening full of the linnet's wings.

I will arise and go now, for always night and day
I hear lake water lapping with low sounds by the shore;
While I stand on the roadway, or on the pavements grey,
I hear it in the deep heart's core.

If you enjoyed this book you might be interested in these titles from **New Sarum Press**

By Billy Doyle—*Yoga in The Kashmir Tradition, The Mirage of Separation, Ocean of Silence*

By Jean Klein—*Transmission of the Flame, The Ease of Being, Open to the Unknown, Beyond Knowledge, The Book of Listening, I Am, Who Am I?, Be Who You Are, Living Truth*

By Robert Saltzman—*Depending on No-Thing* and *The Ten Thousand Things*

Joan Tollifson—*Death: The End of Self-Improvement* and *Awake in the Heartland*

By Shiv Sengupta—*Advaitaholics Anonymous Vol.I - III*

Mike Kewley—*The Treasure House*

Amoda Maa Jeevan—*Embodied Enlightenment*

Various authors—*Real World Nonduality: Reports From The Field*

Jeff Foster—*The Joy of True Meditation*

Darryl Bailey—*What the...A Conversation About Living*

Karin Visser—*The Freedom to Love: The Life and Vision of Catherine Harding*

Kavitha Chinnaiyan—*Glorious Alchemy*

Suzanne Segal—*Collision with the Infinite*

Han van den Boogaard—*Looking Through God's Eyes*

the forest at night;
I call out – no god replies
there is Nothing there

Printed in Dunstable, United Kingdom